MW01289236

Meghan,

OMG! You are go
to be my new best
friend! I'm so excited
for our relationship and
so happy we met and
can talk about books
and Jesus together!
Can't wait for conference!
Hope you enjoy my book
God Bless you & yours!

Love
Sarah ♥

Seeking Amazing Grace Within the Mess Life Throws at Us

SARAH SMART

Copyright © 2018 Sarah Smart.

All rights reserved. No part of this book may be used or reproduced by any means, graphic, electronic, or mechanical, including photocopying, recording, taping or by any information storage retrieval system without the written permission of the author except in the case of brief quotations embodied in critical articles and reviews.

Scripture taken from the New King James Version®. Copyright © 1982 by Thomas Nelson. Used by permission. All rights reserved.

Scripture taken from the NEW AMERICAN STANDARD BIBLE®, Copyright © 1960, 1962, 1963, 1968, 1971, 1972, 1973, 1975, 1977, 1995 by The Lockman Foundation. Used by permission.

WestBow Press books may be ordered through booksellers or by contacting:

WestBow Press
A Division of Thomas Nelson & Zondervan
1663 Liberty Drive
Bloomington, IN 47403
www.westbowpress.com
1 (866) 928-1240

Because of the dynamic nature of the Internet, any web addresses or links contained in this book may have changed since publication and may no longer be valid. The views expressed in this work are solely those of the author and do not necessarily reflect the views of the publisher, and the publisher hereby disclaims any responsibility for them.

Any people depicted in stock imagery provided by Getty Images are models, and such images are being used for illustrative purposes only.
Certain stock imagery © Getty Images.

ISBN: 978-1-9736-4125-4 (sc)
ISBN: 978-1-9736-4126-1 (e)

Library of Congress Control Number: 2018911564

Print information available on the last page.

WestBow Press rev. date: 10/08/2018

"Reading this book as a fellow cancer survivor, it allowed me to process through some areas of my own journey that I had not allowed God to touch. Sarah beautifully captures what walking through cancer looks and feels like. Her honesty and vulnerability is an inspiration. This is a glorious testimony of how God can use something meant for harm and turn it to good!" - Rev. Emily Christopher Nagle

"Sarah provides a raw and insightful look at her personal journey toward peace with God in the midst of sickness, a peace, as she describes, that can only be found in a personal relationship with Jesus Christ." - Dr. Mark Golden

Contents

Music List

(Available on Spotify, iTunes, Google Play,
YouTube and wherever music is sold.)

Lord, I Need You- Chris Tomlin

Take my Hand, Precious Lord- Joey+Rory Feek

Redeemed- Big Daddy Weave

Be Thou My Vision- Audrey Assad

Write Your story- Francesca Battistelli

More than Anything- Natalie Grant

In the Time that You Gave Me- Joey+Rory Feek

It is Well- Kristen DiMarco

Amazing Grace- Chris Tomlin or Classical Hymn

Come Thou Fount- Hillary Scott and Family

First Love- Chris Tomlin

Alone- Hollyn

O' Lord- Lauren Daigle

Down to the River to Pray- Alison Krauss

First- Lauren Daigle

Overcomer- Mandisa
Trust in You- Lauren Daigle
Here's my Heart- Casting Crowns
He Knows My Name- Francesca Battistelli
Jesus Paid it All- Joey+Rory Feek
You Raise Me Up- Josh Groban
Fearless- Jasmine Murray
Different- Micah Tyler
I Surrender All- Joey+Rory Feek
Thy Will- Hillary Scott and Family
Freedom Hymn- Austin French
Motions- Matthew West
At the Cross (Love Ran Red)- Chris Tomlin
In the Garden- Alan Jackson
Safe Place- Laney Redmond
King of the World- Natalie Grant
What a Beautiful Name- Hillsong Worship
I'll Fly Away- Joey+Rory Feek
Born for This- Mandisa
If I Gave Everything- Casting Crowns
Be Still My Soul- Joey+Rory Feek
Still- Hillary Scott and Family
Hallelujah- Kelley Mooney

Disclaimer

Side Note: I am not a doctor, I do not have any medical training, nor do I claim to. Any and all things said are purely opinion and from my personal experience. My references to detox and my cancer treatment are not for medical use or judgment but are part of the storyline and are my personal opinions, not fact. My references to the soul are of a spiritual nature and an opinion I have formed from my experiences. Anything in this text related or connected to anyone or anything is purely coincidence. This is to be used to comfort someone and/or help people see God's work during daily life and struggles.

Dedication

I would like to dedicate these pages to the beautiful community of my hometown and all my family and friends who have helped me overcome the recent struggles and have been constant sources of encouragement. I hope you find this book as encouraging as I have found you.

Special Thanks to my Editor,
Lisa Clifford
Special Thanks to my wonderful doctors.
Special Thanks to the legacy women in my life.

Foreword

By: Jane Anne Tager

Dear reader, it is my honor to introduce you to my friend Sarah. Sarah is a young woman of divine insight - wisdom beyond her years. She carries herself softly but with intention. She exhibits a maturity far beyond her years, as she offers you this work at the young age of 19.

She writes sharing her experience and journey with cancer. She sees this journey as a challenge, an obstacle placed before her by God to offer her strength. This strength will allow her to accomplish her dreams. Dreams to her to make a change and better the world of those around her so that their strengths may ripple out to the betterment of their communities.

Sarah lives her life with Grace. She is so thoughtful and reflective. Reflections offer her the opportunity to become wiser. This book is a part of her reflection. I invite you to embrace her words so that you may see more joy in your daily experiences. See challenges as an opportunity for growth. As Sarah does, embrace the needs of others and see their needs as an opportunity for you to give more fully of yourself, just as Sarah does. Thank you, Sarah. Your words will help us all live more simply and mindfully.

JaneAnne, a friend, thankful to have experienced your laughter, stories, and thoughts, which are reminders of how to live my own life more joyfully.
Proverbs 24:13-14 King James Version (KJV)
13 My son, eat thou, honey, because it is good; and the honeycomb, which is sweet to thy taste
14 So shall the knowledge of wisdom be unto thy soul: when thou hast found it, then there shall be a reward, and thy expectation shall not be cut off.

I found myself writing this book when I kept thinking about how I wanted to have something to give to my family and friends-to people important to me to make sure they understand how much I love and cherish them. I almost died. I wanted something to comfort me and to comfort those I left behind. I wanted to share the inner sanctuary I have in my heart where God is ever present because life throws messes at us, yet God is always there. I always like to seek the amazing grace in everyday good and bad moments. Once you find yourself doing that, you feel a whole lot smaller and God feels a whole lot bigger. When you understand that, you begin to be still and simply allow the power of God wash over you to protect and love you.

Through every day of pain and turmoil, I would intentionally try to find one thing- just one thing to be happy about. Something funny, something I saw, felt, heard, smelled. Something simple, something incredible. God's grace is in all of it, I wanted to saturate myself in His Glory. I learned I always was able to grasp things better when I was still. Be still and pay attention, God is knocking.

We all have a story. I think it's important to share your story with your grandchildren and with your people. It's like you give a part of yourself to them to keep forever, and in doing that you might just inspire. This may not be a good story, but it's my story, a story unfinished and imperfect, but without a doubt, it's done with intention and compassion.

So many people are a part of my story- so many wonderful people. It did not seem right to not showcase God's almighty power through the godly works of people. My people- people in my life all the time and only in passing- who always came up to me with a kind word or prayer. People who gave so much to see my worldly worries silenced.

My cancer motivated this story, but it did not write it. The tragedies that happened following sickness may have made what I needed to say clearer, but cancer did not write this story.

Our lives are filled with worry; sometimes it can be difficult to not let that worry consume us. I used to worry and be anxious about everything; family members, finances, school, career, future, agriculture, the world, myself and everyone else. What I have learned through all of this is that worry solves nothing; it just makes us sick and miserable. I believe even when bad things happen, if you believe it is God's will, and it's in His perfect timing in a perfect plan, you can push through the normal stress and worry- push through to a realization that God's got this, and we have to trust and be anxious for nothing. You can find me now, simultaneously aspiring for my next goal while loving and relishing where I am right now. I hope after reading this, you will too. I think all things are made for good through God. Worry will eat us alive but, being still and calming ourselves down enough to realize the sacredness of every day and the holiness of God will set us free.

People always wonder what it's really like to have that terrible "C" word if they haven't had it. They wish to understand so they can support the ones who do face it. If you do have that dreaded "C" word, or have had it, you know. Even then, the human brain can block out traumatic experiences to help us move on or we choose to not think about it. If any of you know me, you know I overthink and overanalyze everything. I get it honest, however, a large chunk of my family does that until they can solve a problem or understand something. This story, my story gives insight to that. More than anything it gives insight to the Amazing Grace of God, we just have to Be Still.

Introduction

The Grim Reaper caught me but had to let me go. I had been redeemed by the King of Kings and I was a daughter of the most high, no death shall ever touch me. No death shall ever touch you once you accepted the grace given to you by Jesus. The shackles of fear and death have come off! Victory is found in Jesus, Hallelujah! The fact that you picked up this book means your open to the idea of surrendering, giving all control to God, giving your cares, your worries, your fear to Him.

Sometimes I get so overwhelmed with things that come and go through my head. About the people who go hungry in the world, the math test on Friday. My family, my future, people I love, death, love, health are all things I contemplate. The fact that the world offers a counterfeit word of God and we often get confused about which is the truth and which is fake. I think about the magnitude of God and it becomes too much. I must stop otherwise my head will start spinning.

Sometimes life just gets tough, you have great plans, and you just accept the fact that you are going to be an ordinary person who does what they are supposed to do when BAM-something completely out of the plan happens. It happened to me not so long ago. I was plowing along trying to find my way in the world, my divine purpose, and spread my wings while dreaming dreams of a future with a nice job, nice family, and nice life.

This story does mention my cancer journey, but it's not one of those stereotypical sad stories about cancer or how cancer changed my entire life. I feel like the things I learned through cancer made me better perceive and process things. It helped me understand empathy and understand the power of God incredibly up close and personal. That's not what the book is about, though; it's about my personal understanding of God's Grace and how it interacts with our lives and in our souls. Having cancer opened some doors in my mind that were always there but locked to me- a door that helps me feel deeper, love stronger, be still, and surrender over to God.

I pray each word will be a blessing in your life- that my words bring peace to quiet the storm you are going through and grace to your life you didn't even realize you needed. I hope to bring you closer to your relationship with God and your soul. I pray you will be transformed and your chains will be set free by the Word of God. I would like you to take these chapters, relate them back to your life experiences, and delve deep to realize you were never alone, that fear should never rule you because God has your back 24/7.

All my life I have loved good mood music to align with the story being told whether it was a great theme song for my favorite show or action movie or music I played on my phone while I was deep into the pages of a book. I think mood music sets the tone and makes us feel more than were normally would. That is why I love playing the piano for people; it helps people feel good. At church we always start off the service with this sweet prelude. It sets a reverent tone for the whole service; it calms the chatter and lets people know we are ready to start. I would like each chapter to be like the start of a service and the music to be the prelude to center your mind to receive the words I have written just for you.

You may also listen in the middle of the chapter or at the end if you prefer.

I suggest a certain way to use this book, but of course, you are free to skip or linger or go in any way you would like; however, I suggest taking each chapter and listening to the music I have recommended to set the tone for the words you are about to receive. Each chapter I have given you music to compliment the tone and scripture to support my text that has inspired what I am about to tell you. I also include a little prayer as a guide for your personal prayer, think of it as a miniature devotional prayer for you in that moment of your day. I hope you curl up on your favorite spot in or out of the house. Enjoy these pages and read along with your friends and by yourself as you search for God's Grace in your life.

God Bless You and Yours,
XOXO
Sarah K. Smart

CHAPTER

ONE

Sweet Tea and Giggles

Songs: Lord I Need You- Chris Tomlin and Take My Hand, Precious Lord- Joey & Rory Feek

Scripture: John 3:16 (NKJV)For God so loved the world that He gave His only begotten Son, that whoever believes in Him should not perish but have everlasting life.

Prayer: Dear Lord, allow me to have a gracious heart. Please forgive me for my sins. Jesus, I am so thankful for all that You have done so I may have eternal life. Please come into my heart so I may know You and only You. In Jesus name. Amen.

Death. It's a funny thing. We try all our lives to avoid it, to slow it down, but let's not forget those who rush wrongly in its direction. However, it finds us, it holds no distinction of who we are. It's not racist, not religious. It doesn't judge by wealth or poverty by accomplishment or failure. It simply is. Fortunately for me, I will never have to face this grim reaper. Sure, I will know it's embrace for a short time, but since Jesus literally conquered the grave, the grim reaper will never have power over me, so I will never die. I simply will breathe a breath in this life and the next in heaven. You also will never have to face this fear because Jesus already sacrificed and rose after three days to conquer death. Sometimes the process of getting to the point of peace can be painful. I'm here to tell you my story. I never thought about death, it was merely something I assumed would find me whenever I was called home, and it would be as beautiful and peaceful as a rebirth. It's the living after the pain that is tough and when you must call on God to take your burdens for you.

I'm not here to tell you about myself, my life or my faith. I'm here to tell you about the Greatness of God and His redeeming Grace. By understanding my experience with God's Greatness and Grace, I hope you can recognize the Greatness in your life more thoroughly. Having that peace with your soul is wonderful.

The moment you begin to see the holiness in everyday life something incredible happens. Your life becomes a breath of fresh air- something extraordinary. The process of morning, noon, and night becomes something to be relished because you are witnessing the small and beautiful things God has left just for you each day. This begins to nourish our soul. It is easy to see God's beauty and grace in a mountain sunset or a newborn baby, but not in cancer and death, for example. However, that is when God's greatness should be most apparent; if we don't see it we are just not being still enough and looking closely enough to notice. It is my hope that each page is a gift to you- a reminder that God will never leave you, never forsake you, and that even stars need to have a dark sky to shine. The struggle makes you stronger and a better person who will one day enter heaven's gate. As we mature as Christians we enter a journey of sanctification- becoming more like Christ. I think one of the biggest and most beautiful things about suffering is that it helps us become more Christ-like. Once we begin recognizing the Amazing Grace in this long rough road we become free from the chains of fear, worry, and doubt. We journey and grow in our sanctification until we are called home to Heaven's gate, to sit at the feet of Jesus. I have begun understanding the tip of the iceberg called Amazing Grace, and I hope you allow me to tell you about my journey and realizations of this Grace in my life that is in your life, too!

God gave me the opportunity of allowing me to become sick and to take things away to make me understand and to prepare me in a sort of "boot camp" for whatever I was destined to do in my life. I imagine that in a way God made me experience a lifetime in a single year, so I could serve Him the way I desired to. I believe that we experience bad things to serve in the future better than we would if we had not experienced the suffering. Now I say opportunity not because it was all sweet tea and giggles but, because I have chosen to look at a painful time in a different light, a light that will lighten my soul rather than burdened it. I never clinically died, but I came close to that new breath of life. My body began shutting down from a rare and aggressive type of ovarian cancer tumor called an immature teratoma on my right ovary.

Let's start at the beginning, I just began my freshman year at North Carolina State University. I was a double major in Agriculture Education and International Studies. I also had several scholarships to help me along the way. This was a long-time aspiration, and I felt God had blessed me and answered my prayers about going to college. Leading to the start of school,

I had abdominal pain and fatigue. I went to my pediatrician about it and they told me it was nothing and should go away in a few days. I started classes and the pain got worse, I started feeling very weak and was unable to sleep at night. I remember praying at night for God to let the pain go away long enough so I could fall asleep, and it did. I understand now my mind pushed the pain away and locked it up in my head, I believe God helped me during those long nights, and allowed my brain to shut off its sensors. I was so determined to prove to the world that I could accomplish college and a career my family and God would be proud of. I did not want to admit something was wrong. My entire midsection and back began hurting, I stopped eating because of nausea and pain. I went back to the pediatrician on Labor Day weekend and they did X-rays and said I was constipated, which was crazy since I couldn't eat, but I did as instructed. I called a few times the next week about my symptoms worsening and becoming dehydrated from the medication. My bedsheets began smelling sickly sweet, and my perfume became gross smelling; my friends smelled nothing. Walking to Spanish class that Friday, I realized something I had been avoiding. I knew I had cancer. I'm not sure when I knew, but I did. Place these symptoms in any search engine, and you get some scary results. The smell-the smell cows get on their breath when they have cancer, the pain and starvation that went on for months, and then the loss of weight and the swelling of my abdomen all pointed to cancer.

I went to the ER that day, and they confirmed my suspicions. I was to have emergency surgery as soon as some specialists looked at me that next Monday. I shattered into a million pieces but was the epitome of calm because for some reason, whether it was from God or from some strength I didn't know I had or both, I didn't panic. My ER doctor and nurses were so kind;

they were heaven-sent because they prayed with me and even practiced with me on how I was going to tell my sweet momma I was sick. I decided to keep the serious cancer part out of my conversations with family, not wanting to upset people. That weekend I got all my paperwork in line with school, and I gathered documents of ideas I had to help the world and my wishes for things if I was called home. I gave these to Jane Anne, a trusted friend. These things were ideas for a non-profit and things I wanted to see solved in the world; ideas I had for problems with agriculture, water, hunger and ministry. I gave a list of things I wanted to accomplish, to experience. I wanted someone else to be given a chance to do what I could not. I trusted Jane Anne to find that person or persons. A girl down the hall from my dorm who was an atheist went to the store and later packed my bag for the hospital. Two friends I met at church brought me food and comfort that weekend while I waited for my parents to make the drive to Raleigh. This just goes to show anyone can be kind, and it's our job to be kind back and let God lead us and take care of the rest.

We went through with a little hassle, but eventually God made sure I had the best doctors in Chapel Hill to care for me. I remember calling and telling my close friends and family the news of my sickness- so afraid people would not know that I loved them dearly- so regretful of the things I wouldn't get to do or experience- so afraid to face this monster called cancer- so afraid to have my entire life crippled by this evil thing. Understanding that death is a rebirth and actually feeling it is very different, and it took me a few days to get myself and my thoughts organized on the matter, but by the time a few days passed, I was ready to go. The pain so bad I just wanted it to go away; I was so very tired.

I have never been the patient in a hospital, no surgeries or illnesses. I never even had an IV. The haunting echo of the beeping machines and background chatter of the nurses rushing around faded into the back of my mind as I began to try to process the truth of my situation. Everything I have done and haven't got the chance to do. I had no regrets except I would not get to experience life the way other young women get to. Usually the heart rate skyrockets when you are under stress however moment by moment my heart rate slowed until I was under 30 beats per minute. Slower and slower I began to feel light.

As I laid there in what possibly might be my death bed in pain and so tired, I prayed for so many things. Dreams and people in my life, I prayed for myself to live for God to help me and then asked if I did go to heaven that Jesus would hold my hand when it happened and then would stay with my family to comfort them. To be very honest, I hardly prayed these things; they were in my heart, and I had mentioned them to Jesus. Praying at that time was too hard, too emotional and required energy I didn't have. I remember lying in bed and a floating sensation came over me- a sense of peace. I knew that it was because Jesus sat on the foot of my bed. I looked over at my momma and told her no matter what happens I love her, and that I might get to see Jesus, and that everyone should be jealous that I get to see Him first.

That very same night my only living grandfather passed away suddenly from an aneurysm. He was relatively healthy for his age, and suddenly he was just gone. Everything was so crazy that it was very difficult to feel the loss, to really believe he was gone forever- that never again would he slip me stick candy from the old general store. I knew that Paw Paw was in Heaven and was with Jesus so my heart, though saddened by his loss, was happy he was home. It seemed overwhelming as things kept happening all at once.

CHAPTER

TWO

Humanity is Redeemable

Songs: Redeemed- Big Daddy Weave and Be Thou my Vision- Audrey Assad

Scripture: Romans 3:23-25 (NKJV) "for all have sinned and fall short of the glory of God, and are justified by his grace as a gift, through the redemption that is in Christ Jesus, whom God put forward as a propitiation by his blood, to be received by faith. This was to show God's righteousness because in his divine forbearance he had passed over former sins."

Prayer: Jesus I come to you with an overflowing heart. Please help me see the good in the world but recognize the trickery and evil. Jesus help me see the good in people. Surround me with people that love You like I do. Help me understand what to do when I encounter adversary and struggle. Help me accept the things I cannot change and help me solve the things I can. In Jesus name. Amen.

I did survive the surgery. I later found out that my doctors thought it might have spread to my other organs- a terminal point in cancer. Most of the time I learned that ovarian cancer only has symptoms if it's in stages three and four which are quite fatal in many cases, however, I am in some limbo between stage one and two officially, my symptoms were due to the size of the tumor, nine pounds! That's bigger than a baby!

After surgery, I felt lighter but was experiencing a different type of pain. Cutting me vertically across my entire abdomen was rough. My very independent self-was, for the first time since I was a baby, helpless. I could not even raise up in bed by myself. While I was recovering from the surgery, I was given time to decide what to do for my future. There was something that had been lingering in my mind and something I was determined to do everything possible for, having a child. Being eighteen years old rarely do we have to make up our minds about family and children. I did. I knew I wanted a family- many children from my own womb and adopted. I wanted to give my knowledge and pass on my faith to beautiful children I could mother and nurture in a world filled with strife, so maybe they could help make the world a better place like I want to do. I believe the solution to the entire world's problems is Jesus and a wholesome family foundation. I wanted to experience the most beautiful thing a woman can do, carry life. With the odds stacked against me, I relied on God and my knowledge of cows. On the farm, we can "flush" a cow and obtain many eggs from her to place in other cows, so we can have many babies with the mother's quality genetics. If we can do it to cows, we can do it to people. Later I learned there is this thing called IVF, a fertility preservation process which also helps a woman get pregnant. After I was strong enough to get around after my surgery, I pursued this idea and under careful and prayerful consideration decided to spend a fortune on doing this process.

After my diagnosis, I didn't know, but Carol my piano teacher and other people in my church back home were planning a huge fundraiser. That fundraiser paid not only for all my fertility but also my medical bills that my insurance didn't cover. I went down the road from my house to our local fire department, and there were hundreds of people- most everyone I knew and people I did not! People came out of the woodwork to donate and give comfort to me- for me, some girl who was seriously nothing special. Yet people were giving me money not only to pay for my life, by paying for treatments and surgeries, but also my children's lives. What mother can tell her children that their entire community saved their lives? I have a box of three hundred or so cards and letters that were like little lifelines each time they came in the mail- you see them in some of the pages of this book. All that day I kept my tears away until a girl I went to school with, someone confused about their faith and who didn't want anything to do with children, came to me and told me she would carry my child or give me one of her own if I was unable to. I deserved to be a mother, and she wanted to help me do that. I cried so hard- cried because someone so misunderstood stood here with so much kindness and was offering something so great. We must remember to be kind to everyone no matter how strange or how different because this girl so different from me was offering me the one thing I wanted most that no one else had offered- the opportunity to be a mother one day. It takes someone so strong to offer a gift like a child.

I always thought the world was beautiful and had wonderful people in it, but the bad people outnumbered the good people. I was wrong. It wasn't the money; it was the fact that they came out and stayed all day; musicians performing, dancers' dancing, auction items selling, business owners, farmers, family, friends, teachers, students, and people I had only met once or people who only knew me through a friend of theirs. All of this was overwhelming; guilt began to set it, guilt that people were giving me this and not someone else. There are so many people worse off than me. Yet here I was accepting this blessing when all of this should be going to other sick people and hungry children. I hated the attention, the attention I was unsure of how to handle. It took several people talking to me to convince me it was okay. One of the most memorable conversations is the one I had with a local waitress at one of my favorite places to eat. She told me it would be selfish for me to take away others' opportunity to give so they may be blessed by God in their life. By allowing them with a gracious heart to help me they nourished their soul. By supporting me they were opening themselves up to God's blessings and a stronger relationship. I feel good when I help people, so let those people help you back. This is not a time for guilt or pride. What finally made me see reason was the thought it wasn't for me but for God, that all these people were doing God's work in the world, and this was an opportunity of fellowship for my community. I prepared a thank you address for everyone there.

Thank You Message

"Sickness and death are funny things. We often worry and are consumed with the pain they bring; however, like with most things these things have good in them. You simply must look closely. The opportunity to face these fears and understand that peace will come from them through Jesus is a life-changing experience. God declares that He has a plan for us, and often that includes a plan that will force us to see

something we were once blind to see. These dramatic things give people an opportunity to be like Jesus, and that has been so apparent to me in these times of hardship that the capability of human love is very much alive especially in my community. I am addressing this message to each and every person who has helped my family and myself in their own special way. Some of you have sent cards, some of you have given your talents and time, some of you have given financial assistance, and some have given moral support. Many of you have prayed and many have loved me and for all of these things, I am grateful. I remember you, and I appreciate all that you have done. To those of you at this bittersweet celebration, I would like you to know how confused and stunned I was when I was told my church, my school, and my community were getting together for the purpose of helping me. I believe my heart must have burst with how to overcome I was with the shock and love I felt. I believe I even cried harder then, than when I was in the hospital. This love, love that I feel so undeserving of, I would like to ask all of you if you would make this bittersweet celebration not about me but about God, for what a wonderful opportunity of fellowship this is. The Bible tells us that a church is not a building, but a people, and I am so very happy that you all are my people. Let this day be the day that outshines all wickedness in the world we have seen as of late. Let this be a reminder to us all that goodness in humanity has not abandoned this world but is very much alive. My health has always been excellent, and God had handed me all that I wanted at this time in my life. Wonderful University with scholarships to pay for it, International Travel trip coming up, amazing friends and family. Being away from home only made me closer to God because He has always been there for me.

This was a total surprise.
However, never have I been bitter or angry about
what happened and to be honest looking back now
I saw signs of my cancer prior to diagnosis.
Years ago, when I made a relationship with Jesus and
as years went by and I spoke with Jesus, I promised
God that I was his humble servant to mold me
and make me use me for His higher purpose.
The song "You Raise Me Up" that Carol and Shirley
will play for you today surely describes God's plan.
For when He puts us through suffering he will still
raise us up and lift our hearts by sending angels to
help us. It seems to me that you all are my angels.
This suffering has given me the opportunity to be unafraid
of death, more fearless in my faith than I ever was before.
I know God will see good come out of this painful
and long journey, all we must do is wait to see it.
Again, I thank you for loving me like Jesus and helping
me pay for my medical treatments and medications.
I hope to take this memory of the overwhelming love
I feel from God and from my home, from the people
that make this place home and pay it forward to
someone else once I'm back in fighting form.
Perhaps sharing my story more communities
will become as compassionate as mine.
A person never truly knows they are loved until something
terrible happens, so I thank you, thank you with all
my heart, and I want to say I love you, I love you for
reminding me what human love truly is like."

I had done several speeches in high school, but none came close to the rawness and honesty I put into this one. Part of the reason I write this book is to showcase the love these people gave to me. The world should know and learn from my community from these people who appear to be nothing special, but are earthly angels in disguise. God promises never to abandon us, and I think He sent all these people, so it would be clear that I wasn't alone. He sent people to help me and do His work by not only helping me but, remembering to be kind to one another. In a world filled with harshness and strife, this act of kindness turned the tide for the evidence of goodness in humanity.

CHAPTER

THREE

The Club

Songs: Write Your Story- Francesca Battistelli and More than Anything- Natalie Grant and In the Time that You Gave Me-Joey & Rory Feek

Scripture: Luke 6:38 (NKJV)
Give, and it will be given to you: good measure, pressed down, shaken together, and running over will be put into your bosom. For with the same measure that you use, it will be measured back to you.

Prayer: Dear Father, please guide me to Your will. Teach me how to love those I don't agree with. Teach my heart to remain calm in suffering. Please write my story, be my deliverer out of this darkness. Calm my soul and tune my heart to Your Grace. Allow me to be generous in word and in action. Help me give everything I can so I can be Your beloved. Help me find value only in You. In Jesus's name.

Amen

Following the benefit and my fertility treatment chemotherapy was on the horizon. My hair, long, curly and red was my hallmark. I was recognized and remembered by my hair; it was nice hair, too. I can honestly say I'm not that vain. Sure, like any girl I like makeup and nice clothes. I was no great beauty but pleasant looking. But the one beautiful thing I had going was my great hair. As always, I tried to find solutions to problems. I researched and found a place called Compassionate Creations in California that makes personal hair wigs. I went to the salon and had my hair chopped off and mailed it for a wig. My hair stylist cried with me as the symbol of my detiorating health came to life. It takes about two months to make the wig. The wig would help me envision my health again; I couldn't wait for it to arrive.

The day was here. The dreaded poison was coming, and I was letting it get me. It was either that or cancer. What can you do? Mom and I decided to take chemo at the Hope Center in Asheville, so I could be closer to home rather than Chapel Hill. I walked into the building with the word cancer on it, no one tells you how spooky that is. The chemo room was pleasant, but the people looked sick, and it got to me knowing I would look that way soon, with this look in the eye that bespoke of suffering. The sweet nurse hooked up my port-a-Cath, and let me tell you, you better have some of that lovely numbing cream when they hook you up. That is a tender spot to have an IV; however, I strongly recommend a port rather than your arm, the arm will be black and blue if you take chemo that way plus some of those medicines are tough on your veins. For my look of calmness that day, I was a mess of fright of the unknown. You never grow used to the chemo room, but eventually, you become unafraid of it.

One of my best friends from high school called the Hope Center and the chemo room, the club. I laughed so hard the first time they called it that. I mean, it definitely was a club. Invite only, members-only club, people only with cancer. I could just imagine getting down with my IV pole I named La Wonda to some pop music and Cotton Eye Joe. All us sickly bald people were line dancing and bebopping around. It sure was a club. I went to the club every day of the week and spent about eight hours there usually from eight in the morning to four or five in the afternoon. I absolutely loved my doctor, a Christian man, who is very talented at fixing people who are sick like me. I came to adore each of the nurses in that dreaded club. My nurses called my IV pole by name, every time she beeped they would come over and comment on how noisy La Wonda was. Most people consider my tendency to name anything and everything; cows, cars, household objects, quite strange, but it was exactly what was needed inside that room. The nurses would try to save the single bed in the back for me because I was there longer than anyone else at the time getting Bleomycin every Monday, and Etoposide, Cisplatin all the other days. The fatigue was the worse, like a cloud that hung over me or a ball and chain I had to lug around everywhere. The chemical smell that hung on me was annoying. Nausea, vomiting, rashes, hives, migraines, chest and abdominal pain, the night chills and sweats, the seizures and hypothermic chills were rough, but not as rough as seeing my family look at me with tears in their eyes all the time.

My hair fell out about three weeks after I started going to the club. I had prayed so hard that I would have my hair at Christmas, and I did. The day right after Christmas it began falling like leaves in the fall. After one strand came out, it all came out within three days. I had one good cry, and then I handled it. After all, hair does grow back, and I would get my wig in about a month or so. I thought it would bother me a lot, but after the initial shock I got over it and invested my time in pretty scarves and switching out my lip-gloss for lipstick. I learned from an early age that true beauty is on the inside and in the eye of the beholder, but even knowing that, I still felt like I lacked in the physical department way more than the people around me. After a time, I broke out of my embarrassment and inner turmoil realizing this was a chance to nurture my soul to learn from an event and grow from it. Having something of value taken away to better understand the glory of God, and He is all we need. We don't need anything on this earth, but Him and we should do all good works for Him. Having my daily life, health, hair, and maybe my original future taken away made me realize how small all those things are compared to the wonder of God and His great plan for each of us.

I decided after I started going to the club I would keep a journal of my thoughts and small blessings I noticed throughout my days at the club and at home during chemotherapy. Throughout this story, I tell much of what is in that journal.

These journals are my nothing and everything, my little books of wonder and sorrow of ideas, notions, thoughts, songs, poems, quotes, stories, memories, and prayers all collected within the same pages bound together. I rarely procrastinate, but at the end of senior year in high school, my senior quote was getting the best of me. I could choose not one Bible verse I favored over the other; the whole book is just too special. There was not one I wanted my life to reflect. You see, while I respect many people I never want my life to be like theirs, sure sometimes I wish specific things were the same but never everything. I want to live the life of Sarah Smart and let it be special or ordinary all on its own. I was getting to the deadline, and I saw a notebook that's been on my bookshelf for years, and it said, "Your life is your voice to the world make it inspiring." I didn't know what that meant at the time. Now I know. The journals help me center myself and my thoughts, so my mind won't overflow. They help me remember and encourage me to learn. I hope, years after I'm long gone someone finds these journals, maybe my great-granddaughter, to find that I lived my life for Jesus, my life was my voice, it was inspiring, and they can do the same. However, if my life gets lost that's fine too, I don't wish anything to remain of any worth on this earth. I hope to give all away before the day I'm called home. That I carried labels; farmer, student, career woman, mother, sister, wife, friend, humanitarian, but the labels didn't ultimately define me. Being a daughter of God defined me. I gave everything I had and had nothing left except that one label that defined everything, defined me since I was in the womb until after I'm in Heaven and forever. Defined as the beloved of God. In addition, I hope people criticize me for being too generous; then I'll know for sure I'm truly understanding the act of generosity. When you choose to give and serve others, it must be unconditional. You must be able to give, and not resent not receiving, and serve without feeling unappreciated. Most of the time we do receive, we are appreciated, but those moments when we are not is the time we should rely on God to nourish your soul.

The club is as bad as everyone says it is, but it was bearable, I had a great medical team and a wonderful support system. The sister of my heart, Josie, would take turns with my mom and take me to the club, and she would always lift my spirits by talking about life after all the sickness was over. I love that girl like a sister; it was God's perfect timing that put her in my life at the right time. When I was a little girl around nine years old, I started praying for a best friend, a person just for me to share all that girly stuff with. It took years of people disappointing me until Josie and I were ready to be friends. We were both more mature in our faith and understood the value of friendship because of the bad friends we had both had in the past. That is just another example of God's perfect timing and sculpting taking place in our life.

My mother's friends and family would also take turns taking me to the club and telling me stories about stupid stuff that made me smile and bring me chocolate and books to read. God has perfect timing; the year before I hired a private college counselor from Asheville who just so happens to be a cancer physiologist who later turned into a best friend. It was so bizarre that I had the perfect amount of time to grow a friendship before I needed her to help me with cancer. It's so incredible how my illness made people more comfortable to share themselves more fully with me, and it made me more gracious a receiver in every capacity. A girl who helped me in math while in high school, who just so happens to have very different opinions regarding many social issues, also came and spent time at the club with me. Even though we are different, we can still be friends. I never let her think I was okay with her choices because you should never let sins be made okay; however, I still loved her and wanted her friendship. By being kind to different people and pushing aside my bitterness, I understood that God is the ultimate judge. The only thing we can do is learn from the Bible, recognize right and wrong, and treat all people with kindness.

My family was wonderful. My brothers, nicknamed "handmaidens," saw to my every comfort. They had pinned this nickname over the years because of how attentive they were to my welfare, always making sure I was safe and comfortable. My brothers are true men in a world filled with boys. It's so funny how they are so tough and strong, but they take the time to brush my hair when I feel bad and always are right there to lend a hand, or provide some humor, or protect me from anything and everything. My brothers, so manly and grown up for their age, seem so wise. I know I'm biased, but I feel they are the epitome of the perfect imperfect young man. Even though they are all tough and strong, they understand tenderness and compassion to match any mothers. They were and are sensitive to the proper things and masculine on the proper subjects. They prove that a man does not have to give in to one or the other to have a balanced soul living for Jesus. My father was always diligent in his provision for me making sure I have never gone without. My uncle is always the one to push me to do better and has always done everything he could to see me succeed. I am like his little girl; he calls me that, "his little girl." I still remember how, when I was little, he would take me on these "rosy walks." My mother had big hybrid tea roses around our house, and he would pick the thorns off the ones I liked and put them in a vase beside my bed. My grandmother is always the one I call for advice or someone to just listen and provide support; she had always thought I could do anything. She was the one who convinced me writing this was not a silly idea. My great aunt Betty has always been so consistent in giving me scripture when I needed it and has always believed in me. My momma was the most constant, spending every day and every night with me. She saw and comforted me through things that would scare most mothers away. I thank her for that and will never be able to repay all she went through with me.

The club was my life for weeks. I was someone who had to accomplish something or complete one of my many to-do lists every day and every week, otherwise I felt lazy and wasteful of my time. I loved keeping busy with things I thought worthwhile, school, farming, FFA, church, volunteering, it was always something, but during chemo, my world stopped. Too tired to do anything but sleep and sit around, I felt like a failure until I realized this is what depression feels like. My body was changing, I had lost a bunch of weight, and now I had lost a lot of muscle during all the chemo. I was gaining weight from the steroids, medicine, and inactivity; it made things worse. My body felt foreign. No hair, no muscle, dry itchy skin, you name it. It made me feel so terrible, and then I felt terrible for feeling terrible because I was afraid I was being vain. I'm sure many people feel that way about stuff that they struggle with. To get out of my depression I began writing, something very unusual for me. I began thinking about the reasons all of this happened; maybe God was trying to help me understand something, so I can't let all of this go to waste! What helped me most was reading the Bible about God's promises and realizing that every person in the Bible went through some tragedy, but later overcame it and did wonderful things because of it. Even Jesus went through forty days of suffering and temptation prior to the greatest accomplishment in history, His resurrection.

Forcing myself out of the depression, I had to pray diligently and change my state of mind. I am royalty because my Father is the King of Kings, the Lord of Lord, and the Almighty God of the Universe. We are all royalty because our Father is a King, so that makes us sons and daughters of a King! Since this is true, then that means I'm important to God, and so that means He is looking out for me and doing well even when I can't see it. I need to get out of my pity party, lift my head up to the sun, and praise God because I am alive, and I am His daughter, and that he still has plans for me to prosper!

If you are going through some struggle, don't worry, you are not alone because you are royalty. If you feel alone, if you feel unimportant in the world, don't! You are royalty! God is not only a God of love and grace, but also a God of power and might, so don't worry, He's got this, He knows all things and will do all things for good. When He takes something away,

He plans to replace it with something better than what you had before. I know. I know it's hard to see that now, but He is waiting on you until you are ready to receive the new set of instructions or gifts for your future. These are just interruptions, Divine Interruptions orchestrated by the Divine Himself, God Almighty.

A friend gave this poem by Pastor Carol Crouse to me during the time of my treatments, and it touched me so deeply. I recognized that, yes, trouble will come but my Father in Heaven will always be by my side.

If you never felt pain, Then how would you know that I'm a Healer?

If you never went through difficulty, How would you know that I'm a Deliverer?

If you never had a trial, How could you call yourself an overcomer?

If you never felt sadness, How would you know that I'm a Comforter?

If you never made a mistake, How would you know that I'm forgiving?

If you never were in trouble, How would you know that I will come to your rescue?

If you never were broken, Then how would you know that I can make you whole?

CHAPTER

FOUR

Cow Whisperer

Songs: It is Well- Kristen DiMarco and Amazing Grace- Chris Tomlin and Come Thou Fount- Hillary Scott and Family

Scripture: Romans 8:28 (NKJV)
And we know that all things work together for good to those who love God, to those who are the called according to His purpose.

Prayer: It is well with my soul because of You. Please help me through this. All along you have prepared me for this challenge. My eyes are open, my ears are listening, my heart is flowing. Oh, Lord, I thank you for Your grace and divine plan. In Jesus's name. Amen.

While at the club it was difficult to remain calm and to not let it get to me that they were pumping poison into my body. They have nice ladies who come around for alternative therapies. Basically its massage, essential oils, and meditation therapies. I wanted something to help me. I had gotten books on mindfulness and meditation, but it's always nice having someone teach you one on one. One of the women taught me some techniques, and we got to talking about my cows (dairy farm) and the subject of my teachings on dairy showmanship about how a person's energy and emotion can control how an animal behaves. It just so happens that the same techniques I mastered and later taught can actually be used for cancer meditation. They say that if you can successfully teach someone else something then you have mastered that skill. It seemed God's timing had come into play yet again. I knew how to slow my heart rate and calm myself down, just like when I try to push out my calm energy to the animal, I can make and push that calmness out while inside the club. I struggled every day with anxiety, but after a few minutes of these exercises, I was calmer and happier. Cows and God again came to my rescue.

If you're going through something that is stressing you out, making it hard to catch your breath, making your chest ache or simply seems like too much to handle, I would like to offer you a free lesson on dairy showmanship. Of course, if you are wanting to be a better showman, take this and go to your class! I start by telling my students that you must become familiar with your animal or in some cases cancer, disease, loss, guilt, pain or something weighing you down or something you want to get control of. Get to know it, accept it and understand it. Next, grab a hold of it, and close your eyes. Next, I want you to pick a word, any word, that you are fond of that is easy and short. Words that invite calmness, serenity, and peace of mind. I personally use the word "calm" or "grace". I take the word, and I say it over and over inside my head and spell it forwards and backward, and imagine it being pushed out of my body from my heart, my soul, and my mind, and it's covering my entire body. Sometimes I imagine it going down the lead rope and into the animal's soul to calm it down. I take deep breaths and open my eyes; the chanting of "calm" still going on in my head. I let the peace God has granted me sweep over me and the things around me. All is well with my soul. All will be well with your soul. This does not actually happen, but the imagery of this helps you have mind over matter. This exercise time and time again has been proven to work in the show ring to calm animals down, and time and time again inside the hospital to calm me down. I hope it will enable you to calm down and allow God's peace to surround you and replace the fear and anxiety.

I realized then, with a laugh, that God had prepared me for this. That cancer was awful, but God did not send me in blind like I once thought.

From the beginning, He had me experience things while growing up to prepare me for this point, this challenge. Working with cows and being dubbed the cow whisperer in my county prepared me and taught me how to remain calm in stressful situations. This makes me wonder about all the other life experiences I had to prepare me for this season in my life. In addition, it makes me think this whole challenge with cancer is just another stepping stone to prepare me for my greater purpose, like a boot camp, a crash course in life experiences. I began writing down everything I experienced during the last few months- unbelievable pain, severe hunger and starvation, heartbreak, near-death experience, loss, grief, depression, sickness and overwhelming calamity all at once. Maybe in my life, I would have never been able to empathize with people who struggle with those things if God hadn't allowed me to experience these struggles and overcome them.

It's easy to sympathize, but to really understand, to empathize with someone, that is life-changing. I remember when I was in school I would tutor students who were struggling not only with school but also with their personal and home lives and with their identity. Whenever I would try to help them, often I have been pushed away and told I didn't understand. My life on the farm was anything but perfect, but it was what I needed. The farm in its own way was and is perfect and the exact lifestyle I needed and desire even now. Eventually, the students learned I was not going anywhere, and they did better. However, now I can empathize with people and their suffering, now I will never stand for others suffering needlessly. I plan to do all I can to help people who are hungry and who are in pain and heartbreak. I want to comfort those who think all their blessings have left them and their life is over. I want to tell them their life is merely changing, and God is with them every step of the way, just as a father would hold his child's hand while walking up the stairs.

These are just growing pains to help our soul mature and our lives become fuller and closer to God. God's been training me, and He has been training you for your greater purpose. God places us in situations to teach us for the future. I struggled in elementary school on how to read. That's what made me a good tutor. I struggled in leadership roles in FFA and with my faith. That is what made me a good leader and someone confident in their faith. I struggled with people's misconceptions about me and about agriculture. That made me more devoted to educating and proving people wrong.

What has God put you through that later made you more prepared for the next chapter in your life? God is placing you through fire to make you stronger, just as someone places metal in fire and then cools it to make a sword that is life's ups and downs. God is perfect in His timing; you are the sword and He is the blacksmith who made you and the welder of the blade who will use you to fight the good fight. You are a masterpiece in progress.

CHAPTER

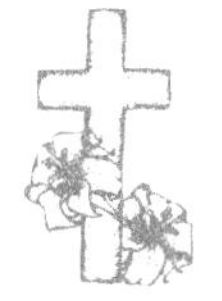

FIVE

My First Love

Song: First Love - Chris Tomlin and Alone- Hollyn and O' Lord- Lauren Daigle and Down to the River to Pray- Alison Krauss

Scripture: 1 John 4:8 (NKJV)
He who does not love does not know God, for God is love.

Prayer: God I choose You First, today tomorrow and forever. God help me love You first. Help me place You before all others. Help me understand Your love so I may love others the way You want me to. Help me resist temptations in the world. God, I pray to You for my chosen partner, prepare them for me and me for them. Help me find my Boaz/ Ruth. I know everything is in Your perfect timing, I know I must be patient, help me hold fast to Your will and timing. In Jesus's name. Amen

Every girl has her first crush when she is little on a boy across the playground or the cute guy in gym class. I never did, and I never worried about it. I was much too busy worrying about other things; however, I did fall in love with someone, someone who saved my life and died for me, who underwent torture and so much pain for me, my life, and my soul. I fell in love with Jesus. When I was a little girl my momma would read Bible stories to me. Anyone who tells you the Bible is boring is not reading it, because there are so many amazing, powerful stories in that book, stories of nearly every genre. Stories of adventure, battle, and romance! Jesus was my first true love in this wholesome everlasting light sort of love. I knew no matter what, I wanted Jesus in my life and in my heart. Year after year I grow in that faith and in that love. I hope each of you if you haven't made Jesus the love of your life that you will soon. After you love Jesus, God often picks out the perfect helpmate and spouse to love you and to love Him and pursue Him with. I always knew God had that certain someone for me. Even though patience is hard for all of us, I felt this is one of those God's perfect timing things. A relationship with God, a being of perfection is extremely important to nurturing one's soul. Without that connection and understanding of perfection in our lives, we will rely on our parents or our spouses to become that perfect higher power. If we do that then we will never have a happy marriage or relationship with our parents or friends because we are expecting an impossible perfection and love that only Jesus can fill the role for. Once we have a foundation with Jesus, that opens us up to receive imperfect loves in our life to complement our own.

We were driving back to the hotel from one of my many doctor appointments right before my big tumor surgery, and I thought to myself for the first time. "I have never been kissed by a boy." At first, I thought this was tragic until I thought, what if I never experience love and marriage because of all this stuff going on with cancer? It made me question if I was smart in not pursuing relationships in high school. Then I realized, yes it was worth it. So many times, I saw both girls and boys alike throw their identities and values away for someone who was not their God-chosen mate. Even though I might have missed out by dying early, I don't regret it. I did a little, but then I realized that I'll see that special someone in heaven one day. I think of the story of Ruth, her struggle after she converted to Judaism and married Naomi's son, Mahlon. Soon after both Mahlon and his brother died. Ruth went with her mother in law to Bethlehem, both widows, both in severe poverty, both alone and in pain. They kept a steadfast faith. A handsome, highly respected and wealthy man later fell in love with Ruth. Ruth reminded Boaz of God's promises after his wife had died after too many miscarriages. Ruth, even after suffering so much and having to go through so many changes, still worked day after day in the field gleaning to provide for her mother in law and praying for God to be with her. Ruth waited, and so did Boaz, and God made sure they met and were able to fall in love. Many miles, many people between them did not matter to God. He made sure that soulmates such as Boaz and Ruth eventually had each other all within His perfect timing. Boaz and Ruth had a son named Obed and a grandson named Jesse who would be the father of David and from whose genealogy would come the Savior Jesus Christ.

God's chosen one for me and for you is perfect and chosen with purpose. Many times, I was criticized for not going with boys, and the only response I could conjure up was the truth. I wanted to wait for my husband. I'm extremely loyal to him because he will be chosen for me by God, and I want him to know that I loved him even before I met him, that I was loyal to him even though I had no idea who he would be. Even though patience is so hard, I think this is one place that it is important to allow God to control no matter what we think from time to time. Most kids my age think this is ridiculous, but imagine all the heartache and nights of uncertainty we could avoid and all the wonderful starts to marriages there would be. No longer will I cower with embarrassment, no longer am I ashamed, and no longer do I regret such choices. I wish all little girls would realize that their worth is not in the admiration in a boy's eye, but in the heart of Jesus.

CHAPTER

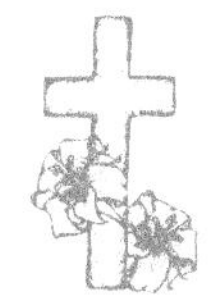

SEVEN

Overcomer Not Survivor

Songs: Overcomer- Mandisa and Trust in You- Lauren Daigle and Come Thou Fount- Hillary Scott and Family

Scripture: James 1:12 (NKJV)
Blessed is the man who endures temptation; for when he has been approved, he will receive the crown of life which the Lord has promised to those who love Him.

Prayer: The road is getting tough Jesus. I no longer want to just survive, I want to overcome and live in Your light. I want to feel Your presence. I hope to one day sit at Your feet. Jesus make my life mean something, help me find my purpose, the purpose You have for me. Help me endure, help me be steadfast in faith. Jesus, I want to be Your instrument of Grace, I want to do good for You. In Jesus's name. Amen

Towards the end of chemo, I was more than ready to say goodbye to the club. They say chemotherapy is bad; take my word for it, they're right. I had grown weaker every day, and my GI tract was so messed up I would have probably been better off drinking out of the creek. My symptoms had escalated, but my mom and I had mastered the majority of them by knowing the signs before they got here and giving me the correct medication to offset such reactions. Honestly, modern medicine is a miracle. God has blessed so many people with talented minds and technology that we now have medications for everything, every illness, and every side effect. We may not have cures, and we may only have things that hurt you to help, but at least you're given a fighting chance.

After all that time spent at the club and having talks and observations with other people, I learned a lot of "secrets" about the cancer community. Some may disagree with what I'm about to say, but this is my perspective of the truth. Some may claim to be survivors, and that is their truth- their perspective- and that's alright. From the very beginning, even before cancer, I didn't like the word survivor. Later during cancer, I hated it and came to find out everyone else did, too. The word survivor sounds like I did something miraculous to get through some battle with bullets flying, like I should be in a war movie or in the armed forces, or something super crazy like living through a plane crash or some terrible accident. Perhaps all people who have really been through something and made it out feel the same- people who have been through some rough stuff- bad relationships, illness, money problems, loss, and depression just to name a few. Survivor is a dramatic word that undercuts the heart of the matter. It makes it sound like it was all about you when it wasn't. I don't want to just survive by the skin of my teeth, I want to live, to thrive. I want to overcome and live! I want to be an overcomer of struggles, and be overcome by the love and vastness of God.

I like the word overcomer; it implies that you been through the fire, but you overcame that struggle to become the person you are now. Survivor sounds like it was an accident that you lived, but overcomer sounds like you knew exactly how you made it through. I know I do. Everything from day one of my cancer diagnosis was really bad, the kind of bad that means a funeral; however, miracle after miracle happened after each and every day of bad news. I know how that happened- God. God happened, and happens daily, in everyone's lives. We just have to be still enough to notice. I remember one day a doctor would not take me as a patient because of my insurance, and the next day he did. I remember signing off on the removal of some important organs if they were cancerous. I remember hydroplaning two weeks after I finished chemo and almost getting t-boned by a truck. I remember our farm burning to the ground; however, I also remember only one ovary being removed, every door but my driver's door being damaged, and the fire stopping once it got to the other cattle barn filled with over a hundred cows. God and his perfect plan with perfect timing is always with us. Going through trial and tribulation doesn't make you a survivor, it makes you someone who experienced life and overcame those tough points in your life to rise above the struggle. We may be weary, worn, and busted up, but we're still kicking and praising. God makes tons of promises to us in the Bible, but He never says that we will not struggle, not be hurt, or feel pain and loss. He says we will not be overcome. I'm telling you today, you will not be overcome! If you think about it, if death is the worst outcome, then actually things are not that bad, death means Heaven and Heaven means you get to sit at the feet of Jesus. What a wonderful thing that would be!

I was lying in bed at the club, and Josie was with me when she was on her phone working on something. I asked her about what she was doing, and she said she was working on my benefit. Confused I reminded her it had already passed, and she responded that the community was doing a second one for me this weekend. If I was stunned the first time, this time around I was flabbergasted. I mean the first benefit was successful and overwhelmingly kind. The second unimaginable in what this meant to me and the community. I didn't go to this one; I was too sick, and I couldn't be around that many people with my white blood cell count so low from the chemo. This benefit was widely successful and was similar to the first except there was a poor man's supper added to the mix. Not only did people still want to give to help medically, but they knew about my love of learning, and my goal to go to college. I had confessed my worries about my scholarships being revoked because of my illness and what I was going to do to pay for my education. It seemed the community wanted to fix any possible monetary worry I had. Recovering from cancer, my mind was soothed that yet again God had sent people to help me, people to take care of my sick body and my educational needs. God had made sure I would have everything I need to pick up the pieces and do His work by giving back as much as was given to me. I have always been determined to give back; you can ask anyone. They can tell you I'm very serious about my humanitarian work. I feel like it is my mission to be generous in any way I'm able. Even in high school I knew I wanted to start a charity to help people, to be the hands and feet of Christ to solve issues that I'm so passionate about. After cancer, it made me even more determined than before to make sure that little idea became something real, something that even when my flesh and heart would fail, and I had been called home, it would still be alive doing God's work that reflects the beauty of Christ. Like I have mentioned before, I want to give everything. I'll be given a new body once I'm finished on this earth so old, worn flesh will be made new when I get to Heaven. During cancer this was very apparent; it made me understand Psalm 73:26 more clearly, "My flesh and my heart may fail, but God is the strength of my heart and my portion forever." (Psalm 73:26, New American Standard Bible) It means what I mentioned above about getting a new body, but also makes us understand that even while on earth if our body fails us God won't. He will be our strength and our fortress forever. Even though cancer may ruin my body and weaken me, God has my heart, and he will send me the strength to overcome; strength to press on and do what I was meant to do in this world.

CHAPTER

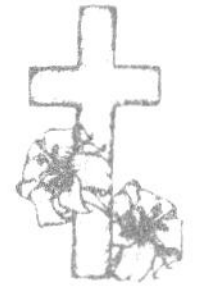

EIGHT

Silent Stories

Songs: Here's my Heart -Casting Crowns and He Knows My Name- Francesca Battistelli and Jesus Paid it All- Joey & Rory Feek

Scripture:
Matthew 11:28-29 (NKJV)
Come to Me, all you who labor and are heavy laden, and I will give you rest. Take My yoke upon you and learn from Me, for I am [a] gentle and lowly in heart, and you will find rest for your souls.

Prayer: Jesus I offer my heart to You. Help me in times of hardship not harden my heart to You and my future. Lord help me not just survive but thrive during these troubling times. Here's my heart Lord, speak truth over me and my life. In Jesus's name. Amen

I come from a long line of legacy women- women who generation after generation have been seeking God's truth and teaching their children about God and the stories in the Bible. I have been fortunate to have such powerful teachers, and I hope to one day become a mother who teaches her children the way all the women in my line have before me. If you don't have a history of having a family that tells you about the glory and grace of the Lord, then I encourage you to seek out both Him and a community of people who can share their stories and who you can share your story with. I know I spoke about specifically mothers and women, but the father is critical in the generation to generation sustainability. It takes a mother to share the truth of the Bible with you, but a father to demonstrate how to follow the guidelines God holds us to. Unfortunately, some of the fathers down through the years in my family have not sought Christ like they should have, but that doesn't mean you, whether you be man or woman, can't seek Him out now and share Him with your children, so they may share with their children.

There is a void in each of us; we are born with it, and it isn't until we heal that void with the love and understanding of Jesus that we are able to later reach heaven and cherish our time on earth.

We are looking for acceptance, and all you hear on the news are stories about acceptance or the lack of it in our world. I'm here to tell you the hard truth; there is no such thing as acceptance except with God. Once you find that inner home you have been searching for and fill that void, then acceptance among people no longer matters. You feel like you fit in because so many are the beloved of God.

We are not doctors, lawyers, farmers, waitresses, nurses, machine workers, but the beloved of God, the son and daughters of God, nothing more nothing less.

Something that ran through my head a lot during all of this upheaval in my life was there are probably so many people out there who have it so much worse than I do.

Several times in my short life I have come across people who have a story that will make the hair on the back of your neck stand up and make you sing God's praises all day long. I think it's sad these people, in this case this woman's story, will fade, and no one will hear her testimony not just of faith but of perseverance in the face of evil all the while keeping her heart of love.

I'm going to tell you a summary of her long treacherous tale of love. Born into a family of nontraditionally educated parents and cruel siblings, she was always put into the corner, forgotten and treated poorly. Later she grew up to be a beautiful, kind, and intelligent young woman full of life. Growing up in rural America in the 1960s, she was untouched by the goings-on of the cities. She fell in love with a tall and kind veteran who worked in security and on the farm. Her life fell into place, and she felt maybe she could make a better home than what she grew up in. She built so much hope into one house, one relationship, and one life. A little girl and little boy came along, and she took to her role as a mother like a fish to water. Then one-day evil crept into her home, evil like she never saw before, evil that chilled her to the bone. Evil's name was Alcohol. Her loving husband became possessed with it. Alcohol was the name of the hand that broke her jaw, that shattered her wrist, that cracked her ribs. The name of the monster who drained their funds from the cost of more drink, evil made sure funds to feed their family no longer were there. Evil was there, and it came to stay. Years passed with no relief to be seen, years of torment, of children living in fear and hating what they once loved. She got down on her knees and spoke to God, "Lord, I don't know You,

I don't understand, but I want to. No one has ever mentioned You except to talk about You with fear. Lord, I have nowhere else to go, please I want to go to heaven. I want You and Jesus in my heart. I want to be saved, but I don't know how to get saved. Please help me; the man I once loved has become evil, and my children and I live in fear. We have nowhere to go- no one to help us. Please help us. Amen.

Soon after that prayer, a friend of her son's invited her boy to church, and there it began. Her son shared lessons with her every Sunday after church until the day came that her son finally explained what he learned about receiving Jesus as Savior and getting saved by Him.

This woman is my grandmother, one of the most influential women in my life. She has made a home that helps invoke feelings of stillness, and she is someone to speak on subjects that go deeper than the average conversation. She is someone to offer comfort and to learn from, who has seen much and has been steadfast in her faith, someone who has helped me so much in picking up the pieces of my life. She called out to God, and He led her husband to the light and her family. She has praised Him every day since. To hear her speak about Jesus makes me feel like she really met him years ago, it makes me wonder what if she did?

Coming from a long line of strong women who have surrendered everything to the Lord, it only makes sense that they taught me a lot of what I know and inspired many of the practices I do today. I remember going to my grandmother, so overwhelmed time and time again, and she would simply say if God is for you then who can be against you? In addition, she would say all things are possible with God. I need only ask and go to Him with my worries and wishes. It leads to this habit- a habit of writing down my prayers, I always catch myself getting so emotional when I pray and forgetting important bits. Do you ever do that- become so overwhelmed with the emotion you feel for God and the magnitude of His presence you are at a loss for words, and you just cry because that's the only thing you can do? Sometimes you just can't do anything but repeat thank you over and over; thank you for the answered and unanswered prayers and for dying for me, Jesus. As I grow older and older, I spend more time talking to Jesus in strange places like the car; sometimes I get so overwhelmed and start overflowing with love and sorrow that I just cry and can't seem to stop. I bet those people at the red lights think I'm a crazy lady with her make-up running and face all blotchy. I have this tendency, so I began writing down specific prayers, so I could remember all the things I was thankful for and all the people I wanted to pray for. Either I read the letter to Jesus or I simply ask Him to know what is in my heart and on my page. I kept little journals filled with these prayers.

I kept journals for a lot of things- things I mentioned earlier in this book. I kept them for my mind wanderings and ideas, but most importantly my prayers. Sometimes I would find myself without my journal and want to write down a prayer, so I would write it on a sticky note or slip of paper and keep it in my pocket to later tape inside the journal. I called these my pocketful of prayers. Things as big as wanting my family business to do better, for colleges to accept me and people to be healed, to smaller things like making an "A" on a test, being thankful a butterfly that landed on my flower arrangement from FFA class, to praying I could find the right words to comfort someone. I would write wishes, and little thank you letters to God. My pocketful of prayers is always overflowing with gratitude and confidence that Jesus will "fix" the issue. Still to this day, I write prayers and place them in my pocket to stick in my journals to later pray about. I encourage you to have a pocketful of prayers; you don't have to write anything down if you don't wish to, but just remember that you have to ask in order to receive. Don't ask for something less, but exactly what you need, and what you want. The only thing God can say is yes or no. I encourage you to always believe that God considers every little prayer- every worry, and He keeps them up in Heaven knowing that one day all will be made good. Keep a pocketful of prayers because when your pocket is heavy, the rest of the world is not.

CHAPTER

NINE

The Sky is Falling

Songs: You Raise Me Up- Josh Groban and Fearless- Jasmine Murray and Different- Micah Tyler

Scripture: Psalm 23:4 (NKJV)
Yea, though I walk through the valley of the shadow of death,
I will fear no evil;
For You are with me;
Your rod and Your staff, they comfort me.

Prayer: God I'm scared of all that's happening in the world around me. It seems the sky is falling, and the burdens are growing too heavy. I walk and feel alone even though I know You are with me. The world is becoming a dark and scary place for me, please light Your lamp upon my feet. Please allow me to feel Your rod and staff as You guide me safely out of this time in my life. Help me be fearless. I want to be fearless in faith, in life and in You. Make me a warrior; make me and mold me for You are the Clay-maker. Make me fearless; make me different. If You will not change my circumstances because they are in Your divine plan and they have to happen then change me, make me different, make me trust in you, make me fearless. In Jesus's name. Amen

Picking up the pieces is something people don't talk about. Cancer in the midst of treatments and illness is difficult, but picking up the pieces is just as hard. Picking up where your life went on pause and hitting play again is hard. Picking up your job, school work, social life, family life again to become the person and do the things you did before your world stopped is hard. You're not the same person, and you are not sure about things anymore; you're on unfamiliar ground. You have transformed into something more; you have something added to you; an experience under your belt has changed you somehow. The most difficult part of cancer was the not doing, achieving or moving. Maybe that is part of the reason why I had cancer; I needed to learn to "be," to be still, and to hold fast to the Lord, to surrender my identity, my worries, my goals, and all my control to Him. It's hard being an active person and suddenly not having a to-do list every day- not moving forward or towards something. It's hard always feeling tired and sick. Feelings of worthlessness creeping in- uncharted waters of emotions and day to day life.

I took it slowly, putting the pieces together little by little as my poor battered body would allow and as gracefully as my mind and soul could heal day by day, piece by piece. What I didn't expect was my world to keep falling apart, for the sky to fall as soon as I got a few pieces put back into place. That I started doubting the old saying God won't give you more than you can handle, and He won't put too much on your plate. It felt like everything was more than I could handle. My plate was running over not with peace, but with calamity after calamity. We expect God to allow us to go through struggle, but to pull us out and say that's it... that's your life's dose of hardship. That's not how it works, but then we expect God to give us a break after something particularly difficult. Then again things rarely work out how we wish they would.

I had just gone through major surgeries, chemotherapy, and the loss of my grandfather only then to get into a car accident, I hydroplaned and totaled my car; everything was damaged except my driver's door. I don't try to test God; I don't want to see if my death is really set in stone at a day I don't know. Honestly I don't test this, but it seemed something wanted me dead and beat down, or something wanted to show me that no matter what God is in control, for which I am grateful. I was uninjured- just sore and scared. I remember spinning and hitting the concrete wall chanting "God please help me" over and over, I called 911, and my mother was so stunned that this had happened after everything that had already happened to me and my family. Only the week before my accident, my father was hit from behind by a car while he was in a tractor. He was stove up but had no serious injuries. It was a miracle.

This next part is hard to believe. Only a week after my car accident another calamity hit.

I live on a dairy farm; we milk cows and sell to a pasteurizing and bottling plant in Asheville. We also grow produce and grain crops. We diversify our operation because the agriculture markets are so unreliable; however, primarily we milk cows. My father's family have been some kind of farmers for generations. Our property has been in the family forever. We have about one hundred twenty cows that we milk and keep in a big, open, free stall barn and have about fifty animals in an old classic red barn where sick cows, pregnant and new mothers, and baby calves are housed. We also store feed, hay, and equipment there.

While we were beaten down as a family and slowly trying to recover and put the pieces of our sky back together, we were still steadfast in God's love, and that this is His plan, and we will do everything we can to please Him because He will make everything good. Our sky fell again.

Late one night our German Shepard, Bran was acting antsy, and my brother Jonathan got up around ten o'clock to let him out thinking he might have to use the restroom. He wiped the sleep from his eyes and looked out the window in our kitchen to see flames encompassing our red barn. He yelled, "The barn is on fire!!" Both my Dad and brother Joseph got up so fast they fell in the floor. My mother called 911. My brothers flew into action, only in underwear, t-shirt and muck boots, and ran over to the barn gates allowing cows and calves to run out. Jonathan was driving our tractor-the same tractor that was just detailed from dad's accident- pulling our cattle trailer that was on fire to move them both out of the way. The canvas roof of the trailer was flaming. The entire barn was on fire. My brothers ran into the sick cow pens and ran the cows out, one turned back, and a piece of flaming wood fell on her. They had to choose to save the rest. They ran in herding cows and carrying baby calves to safety. My dad was getting our big barn and workshop hoses; my mother was directing fire trucks. The flames got bigger; the barn was so hot the muck boots on my brothers' feet melted and made blisters on their feet; their shirts of cotton were singed, the hair on their skin was gone. They felt nothing; they pulled fire hoses to more important places, knowing it was important to save the free stall barn, milk barns, and our home most of all. My father began aiming hoses at my brothers because they were so close to the flames they were at risk of catching fire, not having proper firefighting gear. My mother began evacuating other barns near the fire, barns that contained Roxanne, my favorite cow of all time and others. It took nine fire departments and tanker after tanker of water to get the fire under control. It simmered for weeks after; every time a wind picked up, it would catch back. Animals ran for the hills. We feared for the lives of our family and our community. The fire was at risk of spreading and blowing into trees and homes near us. A thousand-gallon propane tank was burned, but miraculously did not explode. The other barns were blackened, but not aflame. Only one animal died. No people were badly injured. God yet again managed to make a seeming tragedy have solutions and redeemable quality.

The next day the community response was astonishing. People came out and animals came back. Temporary shelters were built and plans to add on the other barns were made. Other farmers donated calf huts to replace the ones melted. People brought materials to build shelters; women brought breakfast, lunch, and dinner for many days after. Mechanics and farmers gave their time to work on the melted milk trucks and tractors. Church members, neighbors, school friends, family, and friends came out to help clean up and repair. There must have been over fifty people on our farm that day. There were no dry eyes either, men and women alike sympathized and understood that could have been them, their business, or their family. Women came out and comforted my mother, who had dealt with so much with my illness losing her father, and facing the blindness of my father's one eye that was stabbed with barbed wire. She watched her father die, her husband and daughter suffer, the baby boys and baby calves she fed every day nearly burned to death, and her dream business she built with my dad go up in flames. Good thing Mom's spine is made of steel. Many women came, called and prayed over us for God to help us overcome this new struggle.

Discovering the gory details of this, I recognized an all too familiar companion- fear. Fear of the what-ifs. Sure this had been terrifying, but I think I cried more tears over the what-ifs. Crazy sounding, I know. What if the other half of our farm went up in flames, what if our cows died? As farmers we take the caring for our animals very seriously. What if our house went, too? What if that propane tank had been fuller and blew up taking everything in our valley? What if my brothers died or were injured beyond repair? I know many of you may or may not have dealt with something like this; allow me to explain. After you have been hit so many times that you no longer can stand, you beg God to stop while thanking Him for not letting it be as bad as it could have been. I know people often feel this way. It took being still and allowing God to speak to me, saying "Sarah this too shall pass, and I will make all things good, don't worry so much." I prayed for God please help me find the calm within this storm- the calm I have had under pressure- the calm I had when I was accepting cancer as a fact. Soon I began thanking God, thanking Him for keeping us safe. I didn't know these plans, but I accepted whatever the Lord gave me; however, I told Him if He wouldn't mind I would appreciate a break until the next calamity. Unfortunately, I asked something, not within the grand plan, but I later understood that the grand plan is higher than me and more knowing than me. I called a few people telling them what happened. People gathered and prayed for safety and guidance for my family and me. I realized pretty soon that everything terrible that has happened has happened in just a way to not damage us beyond repair. I called out to God; He gave me the gracious heart and still soul to handle all of this chaos. When you call out, He will hear you. When you are worn and tired, He will carry you. In fear, He will guide you.

Fearlessness is something of fiction; there will always be fear, pain, and loss, but it is what you do about those things is what makes you like someone without fear. My brothers said it best when I asked them if they were scared when they rushed into our flaming barn to rescue the cattle. "Sarah, I was absolutely terrified, but you can't let fear control you. It's not weak to admit fear; it's only weak if you allow it to control you and your actions. Fear is life; how you handle it is a life worth living." Can you believe those kids are only sixteen years old? I guess you can consider them men after that answer. Sometimes I think being raised on a farm, kids have to grow up faster because the responsibility becomes too heavy for adolescent shoulders.

After everything that kept happening, people began to wonder if we were being punished- if there is some important message God was trying to show us. Perhaps He was making an example of us for something. I will never be able to answer those questions. The only thing I can say is I don't think anyone was being punished. People were so amazed and proud of how well I was handling everything, but others criticized me and told me repeatedly that I should be doubting God, that I have a right to be angry, and that it's okay to be upset. It is okay to be upset and confused, but it's never okay to doubt God. The moment you do is the moment you fall deeper into the dark and lonely abyss called depression. People giving me a way out to claim anger sounds kind to some ears, but to mine, they were burning words, words that frustrated me, because never, no matter what, would I ever be angry with God. I could and would be confused, yes, but never angry. Not only is God wonderful but also, honestly, it's too exhausting being angry in any given amount of time-especially with God. It's not okay to doubt God; it's not okay to be angry with Him. Not only is it an unhealthy state of body, heart, mind, and soul, but also it is senseless to be angry with God. Jesus did not get angry when the Romans crucified Him. He said "Forgive them, Father, for they know not what they do" NKJV. If He can do that after horrendous torture, we can handle whatever struggle we are going through. Yes, it is okay to have moments of upset and confusion. We all do, but this, in the end, should only strengthen your relationship with Jesus. I know many of us doubt, and we have hard patches where we don't understand what it is God is doing to us. Look at it this way, God gives us free choice, and the world just has things that happen, both good and bad. It's God's promise that even though He allows things to happen freely that He will make sure everything will have a purpose in the Great plan for you, plans of intent and plans to prosper.

I looked over the devastation of what was once my childhood, lifted my face to the sun, and turned to the range of blue ridge mountains. I thought that God, my God who made the mountains so perfect and pure, who made the grass so green and the birds sing, surely will see us through this next trial.

God's in control, and we all have an expiration date. The fun part is we don't know it, but God does. All we can do is live each day on earth like tomorrow is our day to be called home. We may not be able to change our situation, and God may not answer our prayer to change it either, but we can ask God to change us, to change us enough to become the overcomer the situation calls for.

We have something, or rather someone, to take those fears for us- to lie them down. Giving those fears over to Him gives us the freedom we desperately crave. What is weighing you down? What worries are consuming your days and nights? What loss have you experienced- health, loved ones, money, reputation, faith? Have you been able to grieve properly and let go of bitterness and anger? Have you cried out to God to redeem, restore, renew, and forgive you? I wish I could tell you things get better; they don't, but how we handle them does because with every struggle God forges a new person who is better than the last, but only if we surrender- surrender to God our Father in Heaven, surrender to Him, His word, His works, and His way.

CHAPTER

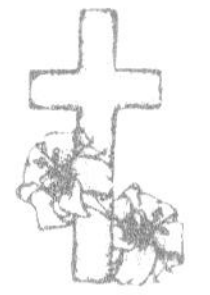

TEN

I Surrender All

Songs: I Surrender All- Joey and Rory Feek and Thy Will- Hillary Scott
Freedom Hymn- Austin French

Scripture:
1 Peter 5: 6-10 (NKJV)

6 Humble yourselves therefore under the mighty hand of God, that he may exalt you in due time:

7 Casting all your care upon him; for He careth for you.

8 Be sober, be vigilant; because of your adversary the devil, as a roaring lion, walketh about, seeking whom he may devour:

9 Whom resist steadfast in the faith, knowing that the same afflictions are accomplished in your brethren that are in the world.

10 But the God of all grace, who hath called us unto his eternal glory by Christ Jesus, after that ye have suffered a while, make you perfect, establish, strengthen, settle [you].

Prayer:
Dear Lord, help me surrender. I give myself to You. Everything I am and can be, I give to You, for Your divine Grace and plan. I give all my cares to You. Help me remain steadfast in Your grace as I desire to do. Help me overcome trials and work against evil's plan. Jesus, please help me be more like You, so I may serve you in the world, but not be a part of the world. I am tired, worn, and broken. I wish to surrender- surrender to You. I surrender all to Jesus. Please help me carry my burden Lord. I need Your help. I love you Lord. Thank You.

In Jesus's name. Amen

I thought I had surrendered to God when I let go of the stress in my life to allow Him to plan my life and my career. I thought I surrendered after giving into God's divine plan and accepting my fate, by being compliant when cancer came and telling God that it's okay. It turns out the moment you think you have surrendered and not felt surrendered is the moment you realize you have not given everything to Him yet.

Rejoice! Rejoice! Cancer free! I had just gone for my final test; my ovarian oncologists confirmed that all my bloodwork came back great, and I should be on the easy road to recovery. I let it sink in that finally it was over, God had healed me, and I could get on with my life!

The phone rang. My doctor asked me if I had anyone home with me. You know that feeling you get when the teacher tells you to meet you after class; you dread it. The entire class knows you are in big trouble. I knew this was bad. My mother was home, and I told the doctor to just be straight with me. On my scans, it showed abnormalities on my thyroid that potentially could be cancer. To make a long story short, it was papillary thyroid cancer which is super treatable and the most common cancer. To most people, this was bad news, but not terrible news; however, I took it very intensely. This is just a warning if you haven't already noticed; this story gets grittier the longer you read.

Hit after hit I took with a graceful heart and gracious attitude, but this was the last block before the jingo tower collapsed. I thought surely- surely, I had suffered enough. We had suffered my dad losing his eye, financial problems, severe pain, starvation, super cancer, the death of my grandpa, heartbreak, surgeries, chemotherapy, failure of flesh, loss of physical appearance, fatigue, car accidents, and burning of our farm. How could God not spare me this? Why not give me the boon of healing I had prayed for? I was a devoted Christian prior to any of this. I was a sinner like anyone else, but I tried so hard to make God proud. I had plans to do work for God all my life. I gave credit to God for getting me into school. God helped me receive scholarships, and I was extremely grateful. I accepted; I needed to be put through this, but when will it cease? I couldn't take anymore. I had been kicked for the final time; I felt I could no longer stand.

I fell to pieces. Gone was my grace and acceptance of my suffering. All this time I could honestly tell people that this was my cross to bear, and I trusted God to be doing good during this time; I just didn't know what it was yet. That attitude was gone. I sat in the middle of my bed and cried harder than I ever had before. I'm not sure why I hadn't cried with such overwhelming feelings before; I can only assume God gifted me with the grace to accept things before. Tears poured down my face; I tasted salt on my tongue. Still, no anger came, but hopelessness, brokenness, helplessness, and weakness like I have never known. I'm broken, sick, and tired of being sick and tired. I prayed harder than I ever had before, longer with more emotion than I thought I was capable. I went naked and broken to my Savior to please save me. I hated those feelings- despised them. I did not want to be confused at God. I didn't need a reason to be angry. I refused to be angry. I wanted the grace back; I wanted to feel free and calm and protected like I did before. I called out, "Please God of Jacob, James, and John, powerful God of Moses who parted the seas. God of Abraham and Sarah, Please, show up in my life. I want You, Lord, so desperately. I want You here, the God that was there for them. God, I love You and I'm sorry I'm coming to You like this, but I feel so alone. Why have You abandoned me? I have been faithful, I have done my best to trust and accept each and every struggle You have had for me. I never have I doubted You, I have always tried to give Glory to You, why God? I even hate asking why. I hate what I have become in this moment. I am a selfish sinner I know, but I can't stop myself from begging You to remember. Remember me, please. So many people need Your attention I know, but please, I need You too! I want the God I spoke to when I was a little girl. I'm sorry, sorry I'm asking this of You, but I don't know what to do. I surrender to You! I surrender, just give me the feeling of peace and grace back. I can't stand this feeling of being shattered and confused. Please, I want Your spirit near to help me figure out what's going on." Tears had soaked the top of my shirt. I felt like I was going to be sick. I couldn't breathe. "Oh, Lord I just want to make You proud, but I feel so alone and lost. I need reassurance. I need a letter in the mail, something I can understand, something direct. I need to understand Your will, to know You are still with me. Please remember me, Lord, please Jesus hear my cry out to You. I cry out to You! What am I to do? Where are You? Please don't be mad at me, I want to understand. I'm not questioning You, but I need to understand now. I need a sign. Please give me the peace, something to settle my heart and mind! Please Lord, oh please Lord, hear me!"

Almost immediately I felt better; days pasts and my peace and grace returned. Three days later I spontaneously went to a friend's church. They had a guest speaker that night. It Happened. God may not have sent a letter, but He sent a messenger. The speaker began his sermon by saying this was not the sermon he planned, but something God told him a few hours ago to speak on. That preacher did not know me, and I didn't know him.

Chills ran down my spine as the pastor poured out words that answered my questions in the order that I had asked, but three days ago. Opening, he spoke in Exodus about the Red Sea and how that God is still here with us today- a God of power and might. He spoke in Genesis about if Sarah had trusted, she would have seen that we can't place God in a box. He can do anything, but it is all within the perfect timing. The pastor then delved deep into Psalms, into the promises that God gives us- the promise never to forsake us, and never to leave us. He promises to always be with us. I realized then, He had never left me, and I bet He thought I was being silly for thinking so which made me think that hardly anyone promises God something because promises are too hard to keep. If God can keep hundreds of promises, part the Red Sea, and see Sarah and Abraham have a child at ninety and one hundred years old, then He can do anything for me, too. I just have to keep trusting. It made me remember years ago when I prayed I promised to try my hardest to allow Him to use me as an instrument for grace and good. I understood and still understand that His ways are higher than ways and thoughts higher than my thoughts. I wanted and still want to be used for something special, something that will help people, and something that will enable me to give everything so when I die I'll have nothing left. I walked out of that church renewed and exhilarated that God, the God of the universe… answered so directly just as I asked. Honestly, I was a little spooked, having the attention of the Almighty sounds thrilling and nice in theory, but in reality, it makes you feel like your parents just scolded you.

Have you ever felt helpless? Felt abandoned? Felt confused? Have you ever wondered why everything seems to keep going wrong? Have you been trying to trust, trying to look for the good, but it's become all too much? Do you want to be used for something special, but then don't expect such intense suffering to be part of that plan? You are not alone. More people feel that way, but most of all God is always there. You have to ask to receive an answer, ask God to help you understand, to help you feel at peace feel grace and share grace and peace. Ultimately you need to surrender.

I realized that once I surrendered without reservation, with no remaining control or thoughts of control, that God would redeem me. I surrendered completely and was honest and raw with God. It wasn't until I surrendered that God could give me my assignments for the next part of my story. He had me endure all of this because I needed to learn things most people learn over the course of their entire life. I ponder if God stuck a lifetime into one year because time is short, and I did not have the luxury of having decades to experience these things. What if God's work requires me to know these things now? I learned all these things in a crash course of one year. I had to go through this to help someone I don't know or someone close to me. I'll never be sure exactly why things happened the way they did, but I do know God is in the driver's seat. My surrender was my final exam, my acceptance into the next step. God never gives you something unless you are ready. Perfect timing is God's timing.

Raise your pointer finger up to the sky. Bow your head. Pray with me. Pray to Jesus that you wish to surrender to Him. You wish to place Him first, first in everything, first in your life, your relationships, your career, your health, your everything. You want to seek him first and keep seeking Him and His truth. You want to surrender and let go, to be free and be completely overwhelmed with His love and overflowing with His Grace and Power.

I encourage you to listen to Lauren Daigle's song "First" to drive this point home. Call out to God and wave your white flag. The moment you do that, you will be free and feel the Grace of God surround you more intensely than ever before. This will transform you and make you fearless in struggle and turmoil because you know God is for you and will never forsake you.

CHAPTER

ELEVEN

Motions

Songs: Motions- Matthew West and At the Cross Love Ran Red-Chris Tomlin

Scripture: Philippians 4:6-7 (NKJV)
Be anxious for nothing, but in everything by prayer and supplication, with thanksgiving, let your requests be made known to God; and the peace of God, which surpasses all understanding, will guard your hearts and minds through Christ Jesus.

Prayer: Lord, I cast my cares on You. Jesus help me give up control. Help me live up to Your word daily. Help me savor each moment rather than allow time to pass me by. I come to You with a thankful heart overflowing with love for You. Help me have peace within my soul and in my life. In Jesus's name. Amen

Many of us, myself included, often get caught up in our hectic daily lives, focusing on that math test, promotion, family dinner party, or church revival. These things are important, and we should be doing them, but they can stress us to an unhealthy point and overshadow our spiritual life. Sometimes it shadows our relationship with God so much that it scoots Him out of the picture or puts Him in the back seat when He should always be in the driver's seat. I, as much or maybe even more than most people, have a packed schedule; school, research, clubs, jobs, charity work, church, career internships and extras, family time, friend time. However, I always like to take time for Jesus, time for stillness, time dedicated to calming, to organizing and prayer.

Never allow stress to take the joy out of your life. Promotions are important, I definitely will want them when I get out in the workforce, but they shouldn't be more important than your family and your moments with Jesus. As Christians and as perfectionist-type people, we try so hard to go to church on Wednesday nights and Sundays, but what we need to realize is church may stop, but your worship and praise of God shouldn't. You shouldn't be a Christian only two days a week, but every day of the week. A common misconception is that worship and praise are the same things when they are not. Praise is lifting your hands and rejoicing with enthusiasm, but worship is a reverent nourishing moment of adding and connecting to that relationship with Jesus. In our stressful lives, we need to take time to do both. Often times I praise in the car jamming out to 106.9 The Light, or I'll go to an FCA community gathering where there is great music and fellowship. However, this does not sustain me; It only entertain me and get me excited. What reaches to my soul and nourishes it is the reverent worship I have at church and the prayerful moments alone and with friends.

Many times, we find ourselves going through the motions of day to day life as Christians. Whenever I catch myself doing that, I cleanse my life of unneeded stressors and prioritize my life and goals. Some school projects stress me out, but I still need to do them, so I take a break and calm down while believing in myself that I can get them done and done well. I like to prioritize permanently and temporarily. For example, I permanently prioritize my quiet time with Jesus and helping my family. I temporarily prioritize a school assignment or interview.

One of the hardest and most important lessons I learned in high school and I'm still learning is that we should try our best, but we should always look to God for the ultimate plan. I remember applying to colleges and for scholarships. The stress started eating away the love I had for life. This went on for months. Eventually, I broke down and made another one of my notorious lists of what I worried about and what I wanted the outcome to be after all the work I had put in, so terrified that all my work would be wasted. I was driving to an interview when something washed over me, and I was just filled with emotion. Out of nowhere, I thought came unbidden "Why am I worrying over this when God is in control?" I'll do my best; if I get the scholarship that will be amazing, but if I don't then it must not be in the plan God has for me. I walked into the waiting room, intimidated by the talented and excellent candidates for the need-based and merit-based scholarships. I realized sitting there that I had nothing to lose and only something to gain. God would make sure I got the money somehow to go to college. I walked into the interview room and each person shook my hand and congratulated me, I stood there in disbelief and said so. They said my resume spoke for itself. I laughed at myself on the drive home, thinking how God must have been smiling the whole time thinking I was a worrying over nothing because

He had already made the mind up of the interviewers before I even walked into the room. Now not every interview has gone that well. I remember walking an interview applying for FFA positions. You know what? I didn't get either one of the positions I wanted, I was qualified, but it wasn't in the plan. I was disappointed, but I did get something better after I got over my disappointment. I realized I didn't need the added stress those jobs required during my already-stressful senior year. I held positions on both officer teams and did basically the same work I would have if I had gotten those positions, but a lot of the work was optional and not a huge stressful responsibility. It opened up my mind and time to plan larger agriculture education projects and non-profit projects that would one day lead me to my choice of career. I learned so much, and God had it all figured out perfectly and offered me signs on which direction to go with my life. Since those days I always go into an interview with an honest state of mind, and an honest attitude of gratitude. The few people in those rooms can't judge or determine your worth- only God can. Interviews are important; I have been in and given workshops about them. The biggest thing is holding God responsible, but with no bitterness or regret. Knowing your worth is through Him. You should be confident because you are of worth, but if it's not meant to be, then that's alright. God will replace any disappointment with a blessing in disguise until we are able to see and hear clearly. Walk into life knowing that either way, you will land on your feet. I remember telling myself over and over that it's a mutual benefit if they select me. They get a hard worker, and I get a great team to work with. If they don't select me, then it's not part of the plan. God knows what you need and what you're supposed to do with your life that will make you happy and help you prosper. The moment you start flying solo you will end up lost and angry, just like I get when my GPS stops working.

Part of giving up control to God is focusing on God so that you are no longer just going through motions, but have purpose and passion behind an action. You must keep reaching to set a goal, pray about it, accept that some things are not meant to be, and that some things are until God says it's a perfect time.

A question I often get asked by believers and non-believers alike is, why? Why does God allow bad things to happen to both good and bad people? Why is there so much suffering? A God of love and power could stop this; why doesn't He? A year ago, I could only answer that I honestly didn't have any idea. The only thing I could assume was God's ways and thoughts are higher than ours, so bad things happen for good reason. This is true; however, now I think I'm really starting to understand the cusp of the why behind turmoil and struggle. Bad things happen on earth because God, unlike any other make-believe gods in other cultures, gives us free choice- the ability to choose or reject Him. The Old Testament talks about how God cast the Devil out of Heaven on Earth. The Apostle Paul discusses how the world is in the groaning pains of childbirth; as time passes the suffering will increase until we are liberated when Jesus comes back to establish the new kingdom. Bad things happen because we are given free choice and the Devil preys on weakness here on earth. In addition, don't you notice that struggle often makes us better people? Turmoil shapes and reshapes us because again and again we go to God and grow ever closer to Him in those times. In a way, the struggle can be beautiful even while it is painful. Cancer was ugly, heartbreaking, and painful, but it opened my heart to surrender and allowed me to gain the knowledge needed to do the works in my divine plan- God's plan for me. If everything was premade lemonade and no lemons were available to us, how would we learn to ask God to teach us to make lemonade? When we are comfortable we often forget God; when we struggle we learn to love God and be better people. For some, suffering can turn them against God, but it makes some people really seek Him and pay attention. CS Lewis wrote in The Problem of Pain, "God whispers to us in our pleasures, speaks in our conscience, but shouts in our pain: it is His megaphone to rouse a deaf world."

Going along with that you can argue that moral and spiritual growth requires suffering. It's hard to be generous and compassionate unless there is someone in need or in pain. I don't believe God causes pain, but I do think everything happens for a good reason. God is the ultimate author; He will craft a story unique to each of us- a tapestry of experiences and tribulation that is beautiful and meaningful to draw us closer to the person He wants us to be. This answer does not even begin to complete the reasons why bad things happen. We can't put God in a box. God is a mystery even though we have a whole book explaining things to us. Could we live in a world outside Heaven without suffering? I don't know, but I do know that if Jesus was born in this world as man and suffered the way He did, then this world must be worth more than we can understand.

People say faith is believing without seeing. I don't think that is true anymore. If you are not seeing God's grace and feeling His presence, then you're not being still enough. All you must do is ask, ask for God to show you His presence. Open your heart like you would if you were a child opening your heart to trust and let Jesus in, He will come a knocking. We like to go through the motions of everyday life, and become bitter about the pain we have to endure and blame it on God when in truth if we but trust, God will make all things good and will bless us abundantly either in this life or the next.

CHAPTER

TWELVE

Food for Your Soul

Songs: In the Garden- Alan Jackson and Safe Place – Laney Redmond

Scripture: Psalm 46:10 Be still and know that I am God.

Prayer: God I come surrendered and with open arms to You. I just want to say thank you for all the answered and unanswered blessings in my life. I ask You to remove any toxic things from my life, be they materials or people. Still my soul and help me find stillness in a world of busyness. Help me be still and simply be so I can be closer to You. Enable my soul to be filled with You and be plentiful and healthful all the days of my life. Stay with me Lord; I wish You close to me always. You are my safe place, my bountiful garden of peace and serenity. Still my soul God. I love thee and worship thee. In Jesus's name. Amen.

I have always done my best thinking outside, close to my mountains and the pines. I often take my worries to my porch, on the top of the mountain in our cow pasture, or to the sitting room of my grandmother's hidden sanctuary of a home. I quietly pray or contemplate something that is on my mind. I often have the deepest thoughts and have a meditative state of mind there. I always feel the happiest after this soul-cleansing meditation. There is something about the vastness of nature, especially the mountains with their unmoving, old, a giant presence that helps put my troubles in perspective. In a way cancer was like the mountains- something that was getting old and making me old- something giant looming over me unmoving with its cruelty. Mountains are not cruel, but they are great, just like cancer is a great burden. It's a good thing our God is greater. It took a life-changing God moment, a moment where a thought comes unbidden without provocation to me and helped me in some way. Unsurprising it came at my grandmother's house, a place that God moments tend to happen more often. I realized things that seem all important in everyday life have become not so important. In the grand scheme of things, all the concern I have or goals I need to see through in a certain time frame suddenly don't seem so momentous.

The scale of the mountains is a reminder of God's greatness and the smallness of our worries. Sometimes it really pays to have a spot for yourself to do that deep thinking and open yourself up to those God moments more easily. I, like any proper southern woman, pour myself a glass of iced tea, unwind, and seek to be still and take in the greatness of the Almighty. God wants us to have goals and plans for good, but we need to make sure such things don't harm the health of our soul and later our body. Think of it this way, God considers our bodies holy temples, so we need to care for them as such; however, when we go to Heaven, we receive new bodies but our souls travel with us. It's so important to take care of your soul because it is forever.

Detoxing my life was and is the next step in my recovery and yours if you are in a time of struggle. Detoxing every aspect of your life- physical, emotional, mental and spiritual- is something we should strive to do daily. I have slowly learned and keep learning how to do this. I recommend effort in detoxing to anyone, not just people who have been sick.

As a farmer, I understand what we put into our bodies is what we get out. Farming is as complicated as brain surgery. Don't let the overalls and muck boots fool you. To ensure all the food we grow is clean and healthy, we simply let our fruit and vegetables soak in some water for a few minutes sometimes using a teaspoon of vinegar. This cleans off all impurities. My family raises most of our produce and meat, so it's very easy for us to maintain a high standard of quality. I didn't realize until after cancer that it's not just food that we should detox, but everything that we use for, on, and around our bodies. I started reading labels and ingredients more thoroughly and researching what those words that we can't pronounce really are and what they do. This sounds like a lot of trouble, but I think it is worth the time, - maybe fifteen extra minutes at the store. I have recently begun using essential oils. I understand this is becoming trendy, and I hate the trendy stuff. I think trends are usually a waste of time and money, but with more research, I discovered some the these self-proclaimed "health nuts" might be onto something with this specific thing. After all, the Bible mentions several of these oils, including Frankincense, which I have begun using in lotions, (Coconut oil) face washes and diffusers. Frankly, it does seem to help. My skin feels better, and I sleep better at night while I run the diffuser. I cannot account for the immune system boosting, but I haven't gotten sick since using it, so it must not be hurting.

I like to consider the importance of food and what it does for not only our body but also for our soul. It is a gathering mechanism- something that brings families together and people into fellowship with one another. Something we like to promote on the farm is farm to table, table to soul. From the farm we know it's clean and healthy food, and at the table we gather and say grace over our food. It brings us closer to God and closer to each other. This results in the nourishment of our soul. Little wonder many statistics say that children who have traditional family dinners seem to lead happier, healthier lives.

As a teen myself, I understand the pressure of our social lives. I've learned even older adults struggle with the toxic relationships in their lives. The first step is recognizing a toxic relationship. Knowing the reason behind your emotions being so negative is vital. I always like to pray about a relationship knowing God will guide me. Detoxing your life means letting go of people who bring out the ugly in your personality, use you, and put you down. I'm not saying if you fight with your partner to break it off. I am referring to relationships so unhealthy that they are hindering your growth towards God and endangering the health of your soul. If you are unable to heal the relationship and God has made that clear to you, that person needs to be removed from your life. People who continue to hurt you and break your trust should be people you are kind to, but no longer spend time with. People who continue to participate in sins that you know you are tempted by should also be people you spend less time with. I love this beautiful example of a friend of mine. After some of her friends hurt her unbelievably she sought out her grandmother's grave. The gravesite was not something creepy, but that place of mindfulness and prayerful meditation. Her grandmother was the person she trusted most on earth. She went there, got on her knees, and prayed- prayed for Jesus's forgiveness and asked Him into her heart. She then asked God to fix her life, such a broad request that so many of us find ourselves asking. God fixed her life by taking every single friendship away from her. She lost her status and it was later replaced with a new status; something better. She overcame, she trusted God, and with time all was made new and good. Sometimes God must take away to replace with better. We must be patient just like my friend. Now she is one of the happiest, most successful and godliest women I know; she is surrounded with a community of fellow Christians and teaches Bible school while owning her own business. We are very close friends now, but it wasn't until God made her alone and detoxed her life that we were reintroduced and became friends. I love to tell her story because it is a powerful example of God's power and plans for us to prosper. By detoxing our relationships, God makes us the happier people that God meant us to be.

I, more than anyone, can get caught up in doing rather than the being. I get so fixated on my work and my plans that I completely forgo just being with God, feeling His presence, and feeling thankful. That doesn't mean school work, career work, family work, and charity work are bad things; it just means it shouldn't be stuff that we place all our value in and that we find our personal value in Him.

I have this habit of working on something so intently it consumes my mind. Time passes, and I don't feel it. Hunger comes and goes, all people and worries are blocked out, and I center around that single goal of finishing an essay, project, or even a chapter in this book. That's why I and we need to focus on God sometimes- to have a moment of absolute grace and peace to seek Him and be amazed by Him and His promises and work in our lives. We always need to have a thankful heart and that Godly vibe throughout the day because it brightens our mood. We need to have an intense moment of focus, of soul time, of God time that is irreplaceable.

Think about the flowers. God made flowers. They grow and become beautiful. We are like flowers. God made us grow up to be beautiful without doing anything but simply being- by basking in the light of His great presence. Sometimes I feel like for every tear we shed, God remembers and keeps them up in Heaven, so we can wash the dust off our feet along with all the struggles and then water our rose gardens so something beautiful will be created out of both the pain and the joy. I think that kind of safekeeping is what helps me not be afraid of emotion anymore.

I feel like more and more in our lives we have less and less time. Ironically my great grandmothers had to churn their own butter, wash their clothes at the river, and pump their kitchen and bath water out of the well. These were all-day chores. Now we have all the convenience life has to offer, but it seems we have even less time than before to be with our family, to learn, to relax, to exercise, and to simply be with God in a moment of stillness. I try to prioritize my goals for the week and give myself a deadline for my jobs, but only if it doesn't stress me out to do that. When I see life moving so fast and stress becoming a cloud over my head, I like to go to my places of meditation to just be with Jesus and say thank you. Sometimes "Thank you" is the only thing you need to say.

I hope as you have been reading and continue to read my words throughout this book that you realize every word is written with intention and love, and that hopefully it helps you recognize God's presence in your life yesterday, today, and tomorrow. You are never alone, and God loves you and will fight for you if you but be still and listen to Him.

We have this terrible habit of comparing ourselves to others especially now that everybody is on social media telling the rose-colored-glasses version of their life. Yes, I'm guilty of that, and you're probably guilty of that, and that's okay. What's not okay is placing too much value on that comparison and feel like if your life is not like that girl or that guy, what you have is not good enough.

Maya Angelou said, "We delight in the beauty of the butterfly, but rarely admit the changes it has gone through to achieve that beauty."

That is so true for people; we comment about how amazing someone is, or how good looking or how faithful they are to God, and to be honest with you they have had to transform and grow, to go through challenges and metamorphosis to become the beauty they are today. It could be a fitness journey or an addiction rehab journey or a journey of financial stability, but what they all have in common is that they have been and are still growing in Christ.

I love vintage stuff; antiques are a weakness of mine. I love things that tell, stories of time, culture, and people. I think about how much those old antiques are, and about how at estate sales a chair is worth hundreds for a scratch and a faded seat. It gives it character people say. You see people take brand new merchandise and use certain oils, grinding, and materials to "age" it. We are like those antiques; the more scratches and hardship, the more valuable we are. Becoming, sanctified by Jesus. Once you have become Justified and accepted Jesus, you must now change and grow like a butterfly, a teething baby, or a worn wicker chair to be sanctified, to be more like Jesus.

When we look at this, sadly we still feel like we are a moth in a butterfly world. After our personal struggles we have transformed into the dreaded moth instead of the beautiful butterfly. What we don't understand is moths are much more beautiful than any butterfly because you must be patient in the stillness of night to see them, and when you do you will notice that they are just as brightly colored and beautiful as a butterfly.

I felt like that in high school and even now from time to time, I was a moth in a world filled with bright butterflies. I loved butterflies and what they represented to me and others, but still, I felt like a moth. It wasn't until after I went through cancer, lost all my hair, my skin became gross, I lost my identity and all chances of being a butterfly, that I truly understood the beauty of the moth. My physical looks, while important in some ways, really were not that important to my soul. It's the beauty of my soul that determines the beauty that everyone sees. God wanted all my value placed in Him and only Him to nourish me. It's okay to be a moth; embrace it if you consider yourself a moth. It makes everything ten times more special because you must be sought out in the stillness of night when God's presence is even more intense than in the goings and comings of the day.

Have you ever thought about how the night is like the lasso of truth that Wonder Woman uses while she fights for justice? The night is associated with evil and sin more so than the day because it's hard to see, and everything feels creepier when you feel you are not in control and aware of your surroundings. The day, however, is just as good and evil as night. Light of day gives the impression of good but can often mask trickery. Do crimes not get committed during the day also? I'm not saying daytime is bad by any means. Night has this thing about it that your conversations with others become deeper and more honest than you would ever be during the day. Being a moth just means you are discovering a deeper, more honest relationship with God and with His people. Rather than being flashy and giving an impression of beauty, you are the real deal- the diamond in the rough. People just have to be still and look closer than they normally would.

I remember all through high school I was so worried I would offend someone with my faith. Saying it out loud it sounds strange, I mean who could be offended by talking of Jesus and His love for us? Nevertheless, I was worried and always made people aware of my faith, but rarely made any statements of anything about Jesus. When I declined to go party and drink on the weekend, I said I couldn't. I should have said that I wouldn't because my faith says differently, but I was fearful of being an outcast. It wasn't until somewhere in junior year that I became bolder and earned the nicknames the "Virgin Mary" or "Mother Teresa." At the time, I was hurt by the teasing just like they meant for me to be. I almost went back to being quiet about my faith, but something stopped me. One day I was upset and talking to my grandmother about the kids at school. She told me to take it as a compliment. Was not the Virgin Mary the woman who carried Jesus the King of Kings? Was not Mother Teresa one of the most well-known humanitarian Christians of all time who devoted herself to others? These women should never be used as words of slander but as a compliment. From then on, I felt complimented every time someone teased me about my Christian sensibilities and called me those names. In my journey to be more like Jesus, I consider being more like Mary and Teresa stepping stones in the right direction. I understand now that high school was a training ground for the world against word view- that you can't love the world and God too. You can love God's people, but not the sins they do. We are bombarded as Christians with mixed messages of the word that have been perverted by the world. All people of the world are swamped with different beliefs and different things that say this sin is now okay and this sin is not. That is why I try to devote my life to seeking the truth, God's truth in a world of sin and trickery. I try to treat all people with kindness, but that does not mean I should agree with their actions and beliefs. Since then I have become more fearless in my faith. After cancer, it became even more apparent that I needed to share the gospel because God was all I had for so long, so it was all I could talk about. From now on I plan to be more fearless in my faith, fearless in the pursuit of truth, and fearless in sharing the gospel with all people to all the world to share the good news through charitable works and conversations over a cup of coffee and through these pages to you.

Are you living fearlessly in faith? Are you pursuing God's truth in your life? Do you understand the world versus the word?

Your soul is not a plant you can water or a cow you can feed, but something you have to nourish through acts of love and moments of stillness. You will notice that any kind of charity or kindness or volunteer work makes you feel good. It's a rush that you begin to crave. I believe God made us all for a divine purpose, and all of us have part of that purpose as humanitarians- people who care for people in different ways by using the skills and talents that God gave you to help others. I have had students ask me and even my own brothers what they should do with their life, and how do they decide what their purpose is. I always respond asking what you could do every day all day long, what are your passions, what do you love talking about, what skills or talents do you have, what does the world need that you can give? The question I ask most of all is have you asked God what His plans are for you? What is He telling you? Have you opened yourself up to allowing Him the freedom to decide? Therein lies the answer. I used to worry my choice was the wrong one, but not anymore. Trust me God will have you going in the right direction as soon as it's time.

That's why it is important to set aside time in our demanding careers, school life, and parent lives to give back in a manner that fulfills your interests or passions but also find holiness in school and work and day to day life. This sounds selfish, doing charitable work for our own personal health and satisfaction but it's not. You still are sincere about the work you do and wish to help people. Do you think it is selfish for people to go to the gym, no you think they are dedicated to their health? Everywhere you look you see replaced food for the soul that will hurt you more than help you. Many think if they have more money, more sexual interactions, a better partner, a better social circle or better body that they would feel complete. What is lacking is not these things, but the ability to see the good in what you already have, to aspire for better is a good goal, but not to the point where you are sick with the want. You need to nourish your soul by building a relationship with Jesus and realizing He is everything we need, and our life is full, full of blessings given to us by Him. We can give back to others, coaching sports, working in a soup kitchen, speaking on a help hotline, giving baby clothes to single mothers. The act of giving and kindness feed our soul because we become as Martin Luther said more Christ-like.

I have noticed after all of this delving into my soul and God moments I have had during such traumatic times that I catch myself more emotional. I used to think crying and anger were unseemly emotions and we should not have them else we look weak, I would look weak. Now I can be listening to the radio and a song comes on and makes me cry, or a book I read makes me laugh out loud and cry all at once. People think I'm from the looney bin, but I feel emotions so much richer, and everything so much more meaningful. I cry and laugh and relax more often now than I ever did before. I am still the type A perfectionist, but I allow Jesus enough room to balance out those tendencies and I make time for the health of my soul that is fed by stillness, Jesus, and meaningful works.

CHAPTER

THIRTEEN

Fairy Dust and Evil Queens

Songs: King of the World- Natalie Grant and What a Beautiful Name – Hillsong Worship and I'll Fly Away- Joey & Rory Feek

Scripture: Matthew 18:3 (NKJV)
"Assuredly, I say to you, unless you are converted and become as little children, you will by no means enter the kingdom of heaven.

Prayer: Lord help me remember childhood faith, help me have faith like a child believes in magic, let me believe in You and Your overwhelming love and power in my life. I'm thirsty for Your word Lord please give me sanctuary in You. Set me free, break my chains. Thank You, Jesus, for all You have done, all the pain, the suffering You have been through for me. I ask You to give me peace that only You can give. In Jesus's name. Amen

Do you remember when you were little, and you believed there really was fairy dust that could make you fly and that there really was an evil white queen in a wardrobe somewhere? I remember my momma reading and telling little stories to me of a man that was swallowed by a whale and a boy who killed a giant with a slingshot and a woman becoming a queen to save all her people. Stories of Jonah, David and Esther were just to name a few. I remember talking to God like He was my best friend sitting right there beside me. One particular memory is when hurricane Francis came through and since our farm is next to a creek we were packing clothes and planning to move to my grandmother's house and my dad hoped to be able to evacuate the cattle before it started flooding the barn. I was so confused, all I could understand was were leaving to be safe from the water, but the cows may not be safe. I was confused as to why all the grownups were so worried, God would take care of us. I hunkered down in the corner near the window and the pie safe in our dining room, facing our farm. I prayed something to the effect of "Dear God please don't let the flood get us, I don't want to leave our cows. Please help all our babies at the barn be safe and please don't make us have to leave them or take them away from their home." We were the only farm in our entire area that was operational and had no issues with the flood. We actually had to milk other farmer's cows for them until the power was back on and their barns were stable again. We were also one of the closest to water, God answered me. I had a childlike belief that something so impossible was possible because God can do anything. It's only until we become adults that we lose that childlike belief. I'm trying from here on out to always have a child's view of faith in God, but an adult's matured mind of scripture and God. I believe we should all try to hold to the faith that is like a child's that way we won't be as likely to cram God in a box that we have designed. So often we see people today pervert the Word for their own gain or their own comfort. So often we turn away from God because bad things happen. When a child would see that even bad things have good things about them. I recently went to the Bible school class of my best friend, I noticed that the children were so thirsty, so eager to learn about God. The excitement about learning the Bible was unbelievable. I wish we could be as eager to learn as we were as kids. The fact is, is we are still very thirsty for the Word of God and the promises He offers, but we are just too distracted to recognize what that void in our life is. Jesus fills that void. By learning and delving into the word it allows you to overflow with God's truth and power and that is what will set you free in a world stricken with struggle.

Do you remember when you were a child (maybe even now) when you would go walk around in the grass and pick dandelions? You would pick bouquets of pretty, yellow flowers and tie them into crowns for our heads and blow on the seeds as we would make a wish. These seeds fly everywhere all over the world, little wishes, little promises, little prayers. As adults, we understand these are a nuisance and hard to get rid of. No matter how much you dig, chop and spray they come back. They seem to thrive even in concrete and minimal conditions. I began pondering this as I gazed at one from my porch. Being still I began to see Jesus in the simple dandelion. He is ever resilient, and He is everywhere. God's Word and power reach all over the world and is always there. The dandelion is perennial, it comes back every spring. Just like Jesus rose from the dead. Just like Jesus will keep chasing after you, you just have to let Him in. It's considered a beneficial plant because the surrounding plants will benefit from its presence. The soil quality is higher, and the pollination is better because it attracts bees. In addition, it is used for medicine, like Jesus the Great Healer. Jesus can often be loved and hated just like this tiny flower. Dandelion comes from the Latin root translated into French meaning "Tooth of a Lion," just like Jesus once a Lamb will come as a Lion. A Lamb to love us and a Lion to protect us.

I hope all of us including myself can grow to be more Christ-like by understanding this little flower. I want to be resilient in the face of trouble. Humble in my life. Prosper where He plants me and help those around me prosper. I want to be healed by the grace of God. I aspire to be like seeds and offer the Word of God to all people of all the nations.

CHAPTER

FOURTEEN

Born for This

Songs: Born for This- Mandisa and If I Gave Everything- Casting Crowns and Be Still My Soul-Kari Jobe
Still- Hillary Scott and Family (End)

Scripture: Esther 4:14 (NKJV)
For if you remain completely silent at this time, relief and deliverance will arise for the Jews from another place, but you and your father's house will perish. Yet who knows whether you have come to the kingdom for such a time as this?

Prayer:
Lord hide me in the shadow of your wings, help me sore with faith like an eagle. Help me be fearless and overcome trials and tribulation. Help me understand Your will for my life. I want to behave more like Jesus did, I want to make you proud. Still, my soul oh Jehovah help me see Your Grace in my life. Help me do Your work in the world. In

You I rest, I trust in alone. Be Still my Soul, I place my life in Your hands alone. Lord help nourish my Soul, help me do Thy will. Be Still, My Soul. In Jesus's name. Amen

The story of Esther is one of my favorites. I have always found it such a compelling story of romance and girl power. Even though women are held in a more submissive role in the Bible, that does not mean that women can't be chosen for something just as special as a man would be. Men and women are equal but hold different strengths in some respects. This is a perfect example of God's perfect timing and your destiny to serve God with great purpose. Esther was orphaned as a child and went to live with Mordecai her cousin who brought her up like his own daughter. Esther suffered early loss, however, she had to, so she would end up at the right place at the right time in the years to come. Mordecai was a good teacher so when all the women were called to the palace to be chosen to replace the divorced Queen Vashti. The chosen woman would become the wife to King Xerxes and Queen of all Persia. Esther out of all the hundreds of women was chosen to be queen, and she was a Jew. She kept her identity hidden temporarily because at that time Jews were outlawed and disliked. Fast forward into Esther's reign there was an evil man named Haman who wanted to murder all the Jews. It was soon realized that Esther had come to influence at a time that was specific to this issue. Esther prayed and fasted before she went to her king and husband uninvited which at the time was punishable by death. God planned all of this, planned for his people to be saved by one of His warriors. An orphan, a woman who came into power completely by God's hand without God the chances of a woman like her becoming queen was slim to none. Esther was in this position because God had prepared her from the beginning; her mind, her body, her heart, and soul were all trained for this purpose. With her beauty and love the King fell in love with her. With her sharp mind, she discovered a solution to the trouble facing the Jews, her people. With a godly soul, she remained loyal to God and at peace with her purpose even though she could die for fulfilling that purpose. Esther decided to trust God and do what he had prepared her for and called her to do. Esther saved her people and still had the love of her husband while serving God all at the same time.

What Esther's story can show us is that God prepares us and then send us off to a great purpose. It might be teaching children, building machines, growing food, preaching the Word, healing, giving advice honestly it could be anything. We have been called for such a time as this, a time to do God's work, work that will nourish our soul and enable our hearts to be filled with passion. God uses everyone, even the most broken of us. The honey bee should scientifically be unable to fly, its wingspan is too narrow for its body. That is how it is with us, we may seem incapable of doing or being something, but with God anything is possible.

I feel all of us have a mission to spread the gospel and to stand up for God and His word. To be like dandelions spreading their seeds all over the world. Sometimes we must go uninvited and stand apart from the crowd. We must follow His instruction and be patient because you were created for something incredible! We must hold our head up high and be fearless! Consider these words the pep talks of your life the encouragement you need to get up and seek God's truth for your life.

In our world today, God's word is being perverted for people's own comfort in what we must do to combat this is simple. Seek God's truth with all your heart and all your mind. I encourage you to look closer at your life to see God's work and to seek Him and surrender to Him, so you can experience the freedom of being the beloved of God. Bad things will happen and sometimes the world conflicts with our faith, but we can fight for freedom!

We are all plagued with doubt in our lives. We doubt ourselves so often and sometimes we doubt that God really is listening to little ole us. Even I struggle from time to time with doubt. It often creeps up when I'm most excited or successful or just overly happy. Doubt comes in and whispers, "I'm not good enough, how dare you think that is possible, who gave you a degree in that?" All these whispers don't come from God, but evil and your inner insecurities. I always like to call my grandmother and share these doubts and soon she sets me straight and I realize what really is going on. However, sometimes that is not enough, sometimes God has to step in more directly to get me out of my doubt-filled thoughts. Just recently I was finishing up this book and doubt snuck in. I kept thinking why am I doing this, I'm not a professional, everyone will hate this and think me an idiot with no talent and no literacy. I was so excited because the words came pouring out of me onto these pages, honestly, I don't know how everything fell into place, it was like someone was encouraging me to write, so unusual for me. Finishing up I thought it was so exciting. I thought to print a few official copies for the people I love in my family and community, but then someone told me to go farther. I did. After all of this began going on, that doubt crept in and nothing could help. I found myself praying to God to either close this door or open it, to tell me if this is His will. Is it His will that I really publish this book to share with His people, my people? I was feeling downtrodden even after my prayer. I began looking over these pages when I received a notification on my laptop for a new Hillary Scott song. The song's name was Still, the same song you see in the

music list. That had a name so similar to my book, interested I clicked on it and the lyrics touched me. I felt like God was answering that prayer, that yes, I am good enough yes, these words are good enough and it is His will that I pursue this. This song was published and released in 2016. How odd was it that in the summer of 2018 I had just noticed it? That it actually popped up on my screen as a notification? God works in mysterious ways, often He makes us wait for answers, but that day He answered mine. All doubt was gone, I prayed a thank you and became overcome with the fact that the Master of the Universe really is looking out for me. The King is looking out for you as well. He moves mountains that I don't even see. He has made a way for me and He is the reason you are able to read this now. Be Still, God will answer. All you have to do is, Be Still.

In these pages, I hope you have become encouraged, fortified and empowered in your journey of sanctification. I hope you are better able to see God's Grace in your life. Life is messy but with God's Grace anything is possible. Go and seek Amazing Grace. Life won't seem so messy then. I hope you see that you can do anything with God to fight for you. Sanctification comes after justification after you accept Jesus as your Savior. We live our lives to mature our faith by becoming sanctified by Christ, becoming Christ-like. When we are called home then we will be glorified and be able to sit at the feet of Jesus, a dream we all hope for more than anything. This is not the end of my story, this is the beginning. This is not the end of your story, it's the beginning.

You were born to do something amazing. You are the Beloved of God. You are royalty. You were born for this. You must seek truth and still your soul, only then will you be set free, only then will truly understand the big and small graces in your life. Be still my doing, be still my heart, be still my mind, be still my soul the Lord is with me, the Lord is the owner of my surrender. Be still and know that He is God. Be still. Be Still, my Soul.

-The Beginning-

Afterward

Song:
Hallelujah by Kelley Mooney

The Gospel

Throughout the book, I talk about my love of Jesus and my relationship with God. I realized after finishing this book I wanted to explain salvation to those who may pick up my book who wish to know Jesus and may not know how to get to Heaven and find that peace that I have.

You may not know the first thing about Jesus or Christianity.

You might know a lot but still not sure about your relationship with Jesus.

You might know and have a relationship but want to know how to share this with others.

Honestly, I think the saddest thing is you hear Christian and preachers talk about salvation and being saved but you hardly hear them on HOW to receive this. That's the thing it's not something you can take or can work for, it's a gift you formally accept and receive.

Well, it stops with me. I'm here to speak TRUTH to let you know the secret, the thing everyone talks about.

These are the first and most important steps you will take in your entire life.

Step One:

Desire a relationship with God. Make sure it's between you and Him. No one can save you except Jesus who will let His Father know you have invited Him into your heart.

Step Two:

Understand what Jesus did for you. You can purchase a Bible or look online at Bible Gateway.

1 Peter 3:18 New King James Version (NKJV)

Christ's Suffering and Ours

18 For Christ also suffered once for sins, the just for the unjust, that He might bring [a]us to God, being put to death in the flesh but made alive by the Spirit,

Romans 10:9-10 New King James Version (NKJV)

9 that if you confess with your mouth the Lord Jesus and believe in your heart that God has raised Him from the dead, you will be saved. 10 For with the heart one believes unto righteousness, and with the mouth, confession is made unto salvation.

Romans 5:12 New King James Version

Wherefore, as "by one man sin entered into the world, and death by sin; and so death passed upon all men, for that all have sinned

Romans 6:2 New King James Version

For the wages of sin is death; but the gift of God is eternal life through Jesus Christ our Lord.

Romans 8:38-39 New King James Version (NKJV)

38 For I am persuaded that neither death nor life, nor angels nor principalities nor powers, nor things present nor things to come, 39 nor height nor depth, nor any other created thing, shall be able to separate us from the love of God which is in Christ Jesus our Lord.

Recognize that Jesus died on a cross for you.

He suffered the sins of the world upon His flesh. He was beaten and scorned so we would not have to go through that. He was the ultimate lamb, a sacrifice so we would no longer have to sacrifice animals for our sins like they did in the Old Testament.

Jesus then rose from the dead and conquered the grave. He made the pathway for us to come back to life in Heaven. We will die, and our souls will be greeted with new bodies in Heaven.

Sin entered the world through Adam's disobedience, and this caused death and an eternal separation from God. God provided a way to restore fellowship and eternal life through Jesus Christ our Lord. Jesus paid the price for all to have salvation through the shedding of His blood and death on the cross. His death paid the price that we could never pay. Salvation is a free gift, all we have to do is confess we are sinners. Believe in our hearts, Jesus died in our place, and God raised him from the grave. Then ask Jesus to come into our hearts to save us.

Step Three:

Ask for Forgiveness. Ask Jesus in prayer for forgiveness of all the sins you have committed. Be sincere in the regret of your sins and be honest when you say you want to do better.

Let Jesus know you understand what He did for you and that you thank Him and want Him to forgive you.

Pray that prayer. You have just become justified through Christ. Your name has been written in the Lamb's Book of Eternal Life.

Step Four:

From now on you have are guaranteed a place in Heaven but, it is up to you if you wish to have more rewards in Heaven from doing good works.

People even after they are saved can slip up, that is when they must simply go back to Jesus and rededicate their life to Him. Ask for Forgiveness.

Step Five:

Live a Christ-like lifestyle.

Bible study.

Fellowship with others.

Baptism- an act of faith where a person is cleansed of their sins in a body of water. A symbolism of a new life with Christ at the center. A public profession of your faith.

I don't necessarily believe you have to be baptized to go to Heaven. However, it is nice to physically cleanse yourself as you step into a new life. Many denominations consider baptism either as optional or mandatory. Christening when you were a baby does not count because you cannot sin as a baby. Sins are only recognized by God when you are old enough to know right from wrong usually around 10-12 years old sometimes younger.

As you live a redeemed life commit to Christian works.

James 2:14-26 New King James Version (NKJV)

Faith Without Works Is Dead

14 What does it profit, my brethren, if someone says he has faith but does not have works? Can faith save him? 15 If a brother or sister is naked and destitute of daily food, 16 and one of you says to them, "Depart in peace, be warmed and filled," but you do not give them the things which are needed for the body, what does it profit? 17 Thus also faith by itself, if it does not have works, is dead.

18 But someone will say, "You have faith, and I have works." Show me your faith without [a]your works, and I will show you my faith by [b]my works. 19 You believe that there is one God. You do well. Even the demons believe—and tremble! 20 But do you want to know, O foolish man, that faith without works is [c]dead? 21 Was not Abraham our father justified by works when he offered Isaac his son on the altar? 22 Do you see that faith was working together with his works, and by works, faith was made [d]perfect? 23 And the Scripture was fulfilled which says, "Abraham believed God, and it was [e]accounted to him for righteousness." And he was called the friend of God. 24 You see then that a man is justified by works, and not by faith only.

CPSIA information can be obtained
at www.ICGtesting.com
Printed in the USA
BVHW031431051218
534856BV00001B/57/P